GOOGLE PHOTOS
MADE EASY

Preserving and Sharing Your Memories

By James Bernstein

Bernstein, James
Google Photos Made Easy
Part of the Computers Made Easy series

For more information on reproducing sections of this book or sales of this book,
go to **www.madeeasybookseries.com**

Contents

Introduction

Taking photos has become a normal part of our lives and these days we don't even think twice about it since we can take a picture any time, any place with our smartphones. Most people don't even own a camera anymore since our phones do such a good job of taking photos.

One thing that many people don't do with all of their photos is back them up or organize them to keep things in order. They tend to just leave them on their phone or maybe use their USB cable to copy some of them over to their computer. Then if they want to share a picture with someone else, they will email it which can cause a problem since today's high-resolution pictures tend to be larger in size and you can only email a few at a time.

Fortunately, there are many ways to store your photos online and then share them with other people without having to take them from your phone or attach them to an email. Most of these services have free options as well as pay-for plans if you need the extra storage space. The question is, which online service is best for you?

Everyone has heard of Google and probably even uses their search engine and even their Chrome web browser. Google Photos is another one of their many free apps that you can use to store, organize and share your photos. And if you are using an Android based smartphone, you are probably already using Photos and might not even know it!

Google Photos allows you to upload your pictures and even videos to their online storage repository so you can use it as a backup and a way to share photos with other people without needing to send them as an email attachment. You can also create and share photo albums with others just by sending them a link. And if you want printed copies of your pictures, you can order them from Photos as well.

If you like to transfer your pictures from your phone to your computer, you can have a copy there and also in Photos. And if you are the type who never deletes pictures from your phone, you can technically have three places to store your photos for extra redundancy.

In this book, I will be going over how to access Google Photos, upload your pictures, share your albums, create custom animations, order prints and more. So on that note, let's start uploading!

Chapter 1 – What is Google Photos?

In this chapter, you will be getting acquainted with the Google Photos app and its interface so things will make more sense once I get into the more specific details. After using Photos for a little bit, you will see how simple it really is and it will make it that much easier to use.

Signing up for a Google Account

In order to use Google Photos, you will need to have a Google account. If you use Gmail or an Android phone, then you will already have a Google account setup. It might just be a case of you forgetting your username or password and needing to figure it out or have it reset. Of you can just make a new account.

If for some reason you do not have a Google account, then it's very easy to sign up for a free one in just a few steps. To begin, simply go to the Google website at **https://www.google.com/** and then click on the *Sign in* button at the top right of the page.

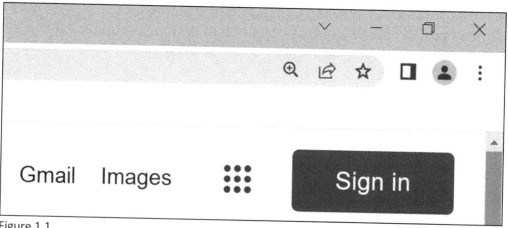

Figure 1.1

Next, you will click on the *Create account* link at the lower left of the sign-in screen.

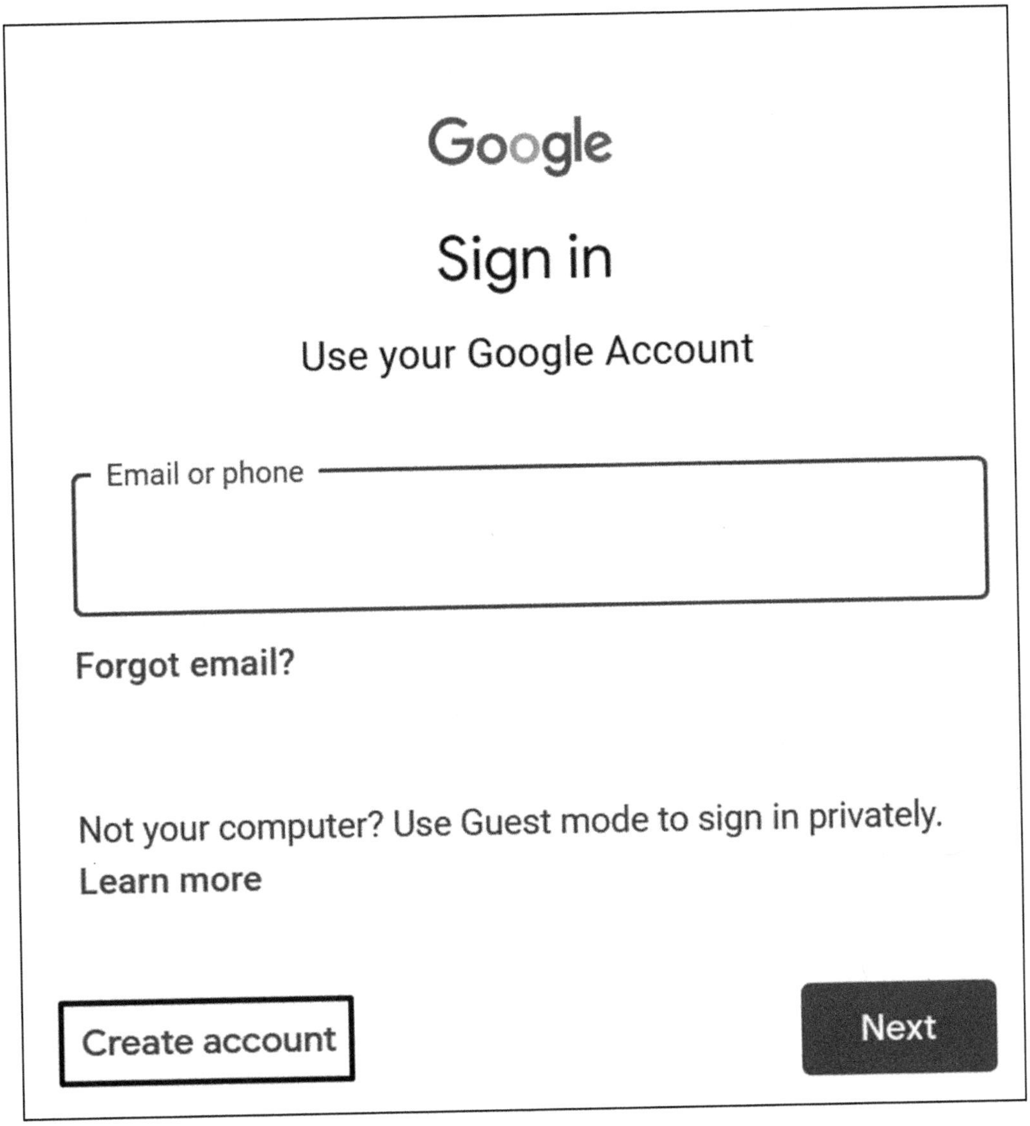

Google

Sign in

Use your Google Account

Email or phone

Forgot email?

Not your computer? Use Guest mode to sign in privately. **Learn more**

Create account

Next

Figure 1.2

Here you can enter your real or fictitious name and then think of a username (email address) that is not already in use. If you do choose something that is taken, it will let you know and you will need to pick something else. You can also use your current non-Google email address to sign up for a Google account. You will then need to come up with a password for your new account.

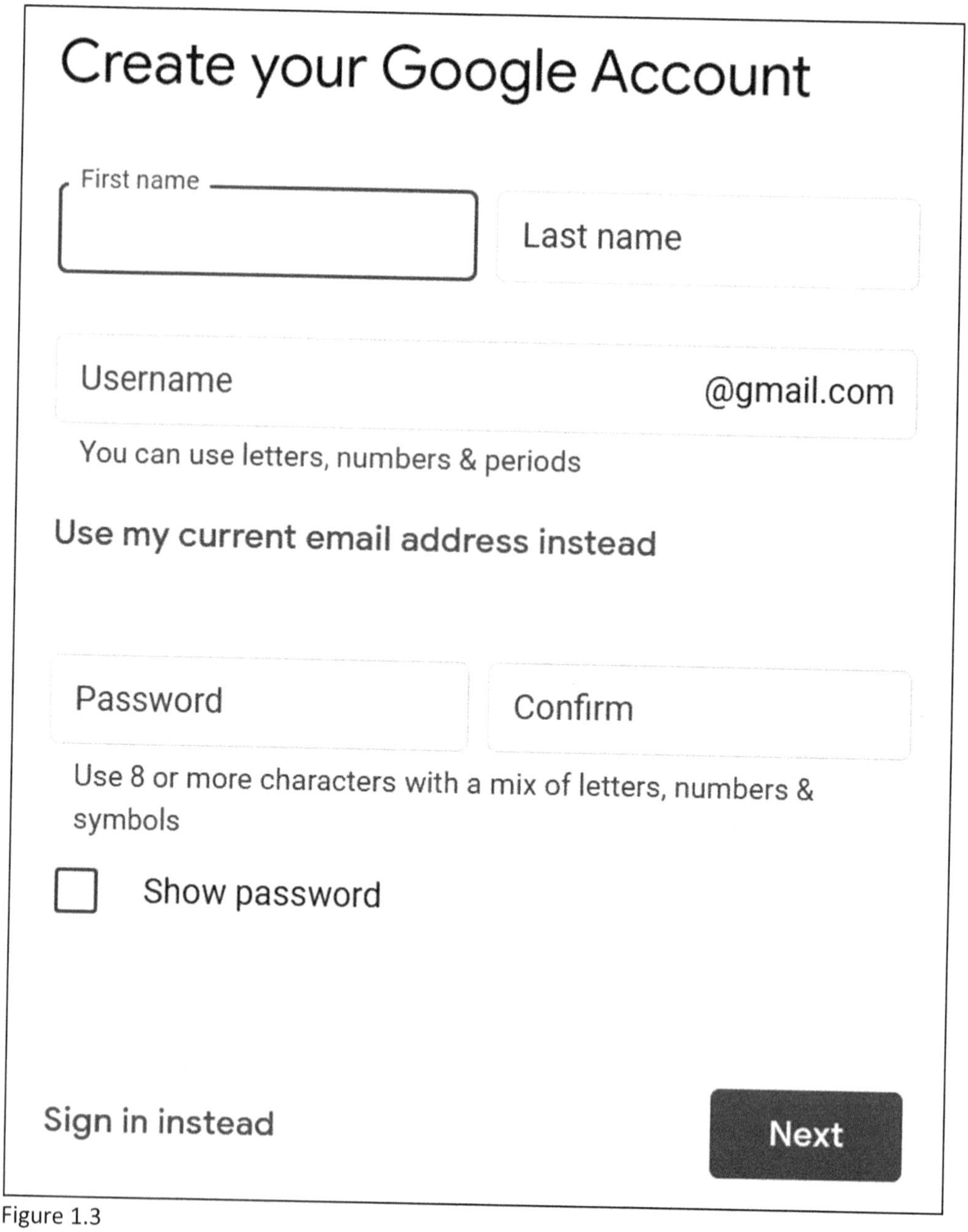

Create your Google Account

First name

Last name

Username

@gmail.com

You can use letters, numbers & periods

Use my current email address instead

Password

Confirm

Use 8 or more characters with a mix of letters, numbers & symbols

☐ Show password

Sign in instead

Next

Figure 1.3

Then Google will ask for your phone number to prove you are really who you say you are and will text you a code that you will need to enter on the next screen. Then you can enter an optional recovery email address in case you get locked out of your account to help you get back in. You will also be asked to enter your date of birth which you can make up if you don't want to use your real birthdate. Finally, you will need to agree to Google's terms, and you will then be ready to go.

Free and Paid Plans

As I mentioned before, Google Photos is free to use but with most apps that are free, you either need to deal with advertisements popping up on the screen or have to miss out on the advanced features that the app has to offer.

When it comes to Photos, the only real difference between the free plan and the pay-for plan is how much online storage space you get to save your files. When it comes to Google apps and their associated storage, they will share the same storage pool so if you use Gmail, Google Drive and Google Photos, they are all using the allotted amount of online storage that comes with your account. I will be discussing storage in more detail in chapter 3.

As of this writing, you get 15 GB (gigabytes) of storage with your Google account to use with any app that allows you to store files online. This also includes your Gmail email account so if you like to keep every email you have ever received, then you might want to keep an eye on how much of your 15 GB you are using.

If you decide to buy additional storage, you can purchase one of the Google One plans. As for the Google One pricing options, here is a breakdown of the plans as of the writing of this book.

15GB Plan
- Free
- 15GB of storage space

100GB Plan
- $1.99/month
- 100GB of storage space
- Access to Google experts
- Share with up to 5 others
- Optional family member access
- Extra member benefits

200GB Plan
- $2.99/month
- 200GB of storage space
- Access to Google experts
- Share with up to 5 others
- Optional family member access
- Extra member benefits
- 3% back in the Google Store

2TB Plan
- $9.99/month
- 2TB of storage space
- Access to Google experts
- Optional family member access
- Extra member benefits
- Google Workspace Premium
- 10% back in the Google Store
- VPN for Android and iOS

The Photos Interface

Like most Google apps, the Photos interface is fairly simple and easy to navigate. It has the same layout as other apps such as Google Drive and Gmail with the content on the right and the tools\navigation on the left.

On the left side you will find the *Photos* section as well as the *Library* section, and these are where you will be spending most of your time. It is where you will find all of your pictures sorted by date as well as any albums you have created.

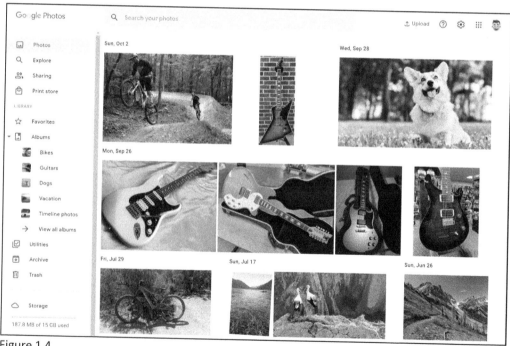

Figure 1.4

At the top of the window you will see things such as a search box, upload button and settings icon which will all be discussed later in the book.

If you click on the icon with the 9 dots at the upper right (referred to as the waffle), you can easily open other Google apps by selecting them from the list.

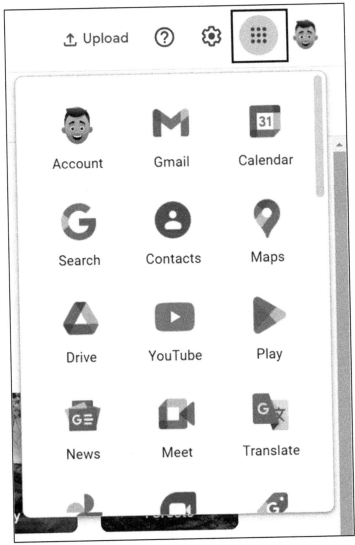

Figure 1.5

Photos Smartphone & Tablet App

If you are like most people, you probably view your photos on your phone more than you do on your computer. You might even use your phone more than your computer for just about everything. If that is the case, there is a Google Photos app that you can use on your smartphone or tablet to view and manage your photos.

If you have an Android based smartphone, then you most likely have the Photos app already installed and signed in with the account that you are using on your phone. If you are using an iPhone, then you can download the Photos app from the App Store and sign in with your Google account.

Once you install and sign into the Photos app, you will see that it looks very similar to the Photos website on your computer. There will be one difference that you might notice depending on how you have your Photos app configured. As you can see in figure 1.6, the app shows a section called *Photos on device.* These pictures are on the phone yet not stored within Photos because there is a setting that you can change so your phone doesn't automatically backup every picture you take online to your Photos account. Most Android phones will have this enabled so you might want to disable this if you want to control which photos are stored online. To disable this feature, you can tap on your account picture or letter and then on *Turn off backup* (figure 1.7).

*If you would like to learn how to make the most of your Android smartphone, then check out my books titled **Android Smartphones Made** Easy and **Android Smartphones for Seniors Made Easy**. https://www.amazon.com/dp/1086026837 https://www.amazon.com/dp/B0B14FW7JW*

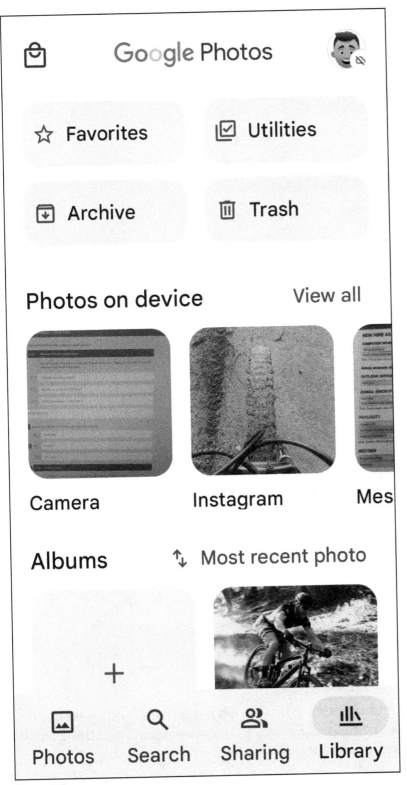

Figure 1.6

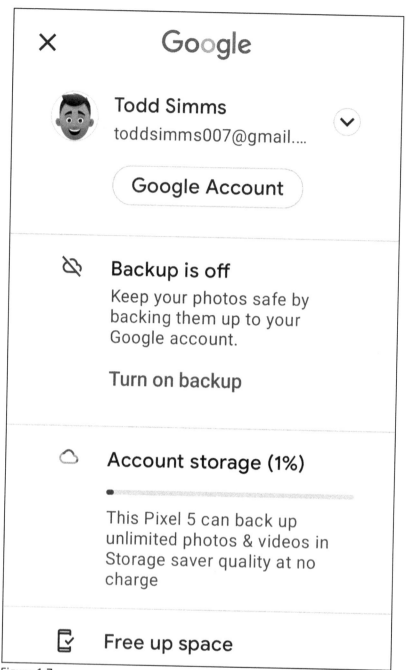

Figure 1.7

You will also notice that the albums on your phone or tablet will be identical to what you see on your computer (figure 1.8). I will be discussing how to create albums and move pictures into them in chapter 2.

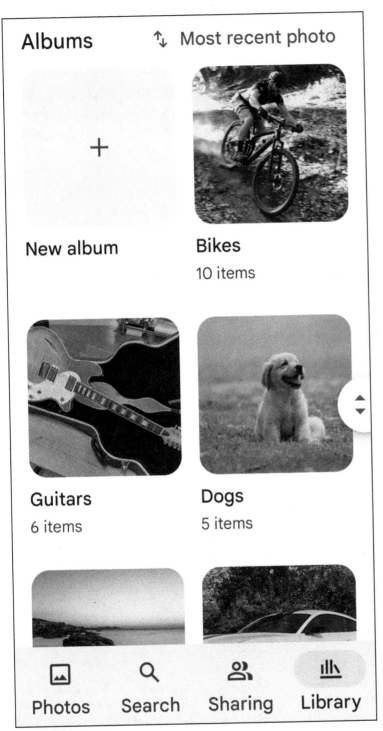

Figure 1.8

Once you get the hang of the Photos website interface, you will find that the phone app works in a similar fashion, and you shouldn't have a problem using both seamlessly.

Chapter 2 – Adding Photos

Now that you have your Google Photos account configured, you will want to start uploading photos and creating albums to get things organized. If you have a lot of pictures, it might take some time to get everything the way you like it in their own albums. But once you get things in place, you will find that it is much easier to manage and share your photos.

Uploading Photos

In order to use Google Photos with your pictures, you will first need to upload them to your Photos account. This can be done several different ways but for the most part you will click on the *Upload* button as seen in figure 2.1

Figure 2.1

This will give you several upload options but for the most part you will probably be using either the *Computer* method or the *Google Drive* method.

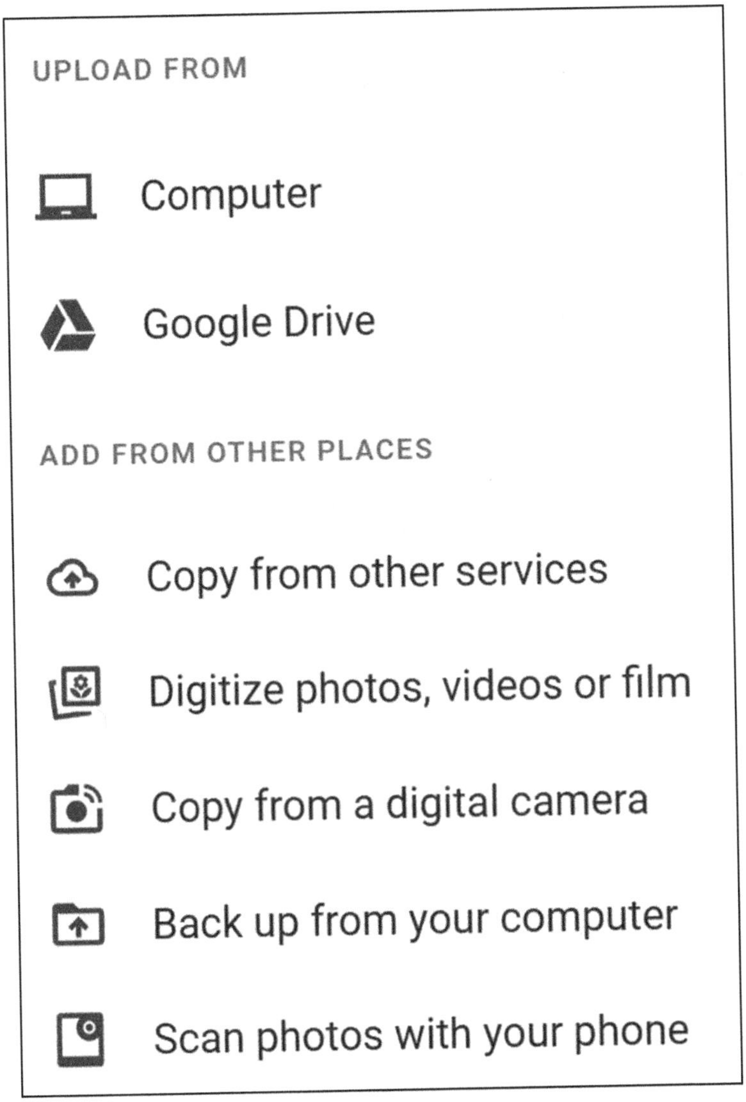

UPLOAD FROM

🖥 Computer

△ Google Drive

ADD FROM OTHER PLACES

☁ Copy from other services

🖼 Digitize photos, videos or film

📷 Copy from a digital camera

📁 Back up from your computer

📇 Scan photos with your phone

Figure 2.2

When using the computer method, you will be prompted to browse to the location on your hard drive where you have your photos stored and then choose the ones you want to upload.

If your goal is to upload photos from your phone, you will probably want to do this process from your phone rather than transfer your photos to your computer first, unless you like to have a copy there as well.

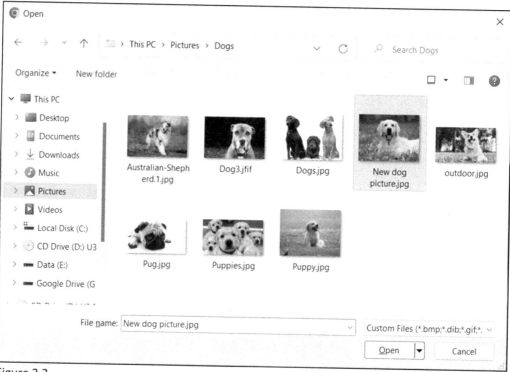

Figure 2.3

The other option for Google Drive will let you select a photo from your online Drive account to transfer into your Photos account.

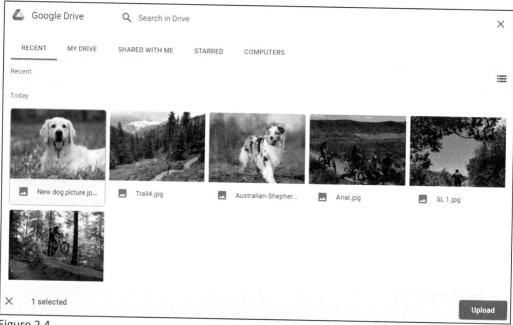

Figure 2.4

 *If you would like to learn how to backup and share your files with others online, then check out my book **Google Drive Made Easy**. https://www.amazon.com/dp/B0BBY4D6FQ*

Google Photos and Google Drive used to sync with each other where you would see a Google Photos folder in your Drive account. As of July 2019, they no longer sync but if you have had an account before that, you might still have a Google Photos folder in your Drive account.

Depending on the method you have selected to upload your photo, you may be asked if you wish to add it to one of the albums you have created in your account (albums will be discussed later in this chapter).

Figure 2.5

If you do choose to do this, you can simply select the album from your list of albums and the photo will be placed into that album. You will also be able to see the photo when you are in the main Photos view.

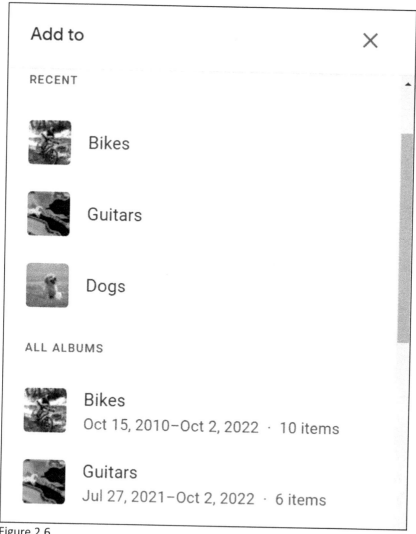

Figure 2.6

Editing Photo Dates & Locations

One thing you might notice when you upload photos is that they are not always shown with the date that you uploaded them. This is most likely because they had the date (and location) embedded in the image file when the picture was taken. Figure 2.7 shows the dog image that I just uploaded but as you can see, it's shown with an earlier date (July 22nd) than the latest photos I have in my main Photos section.

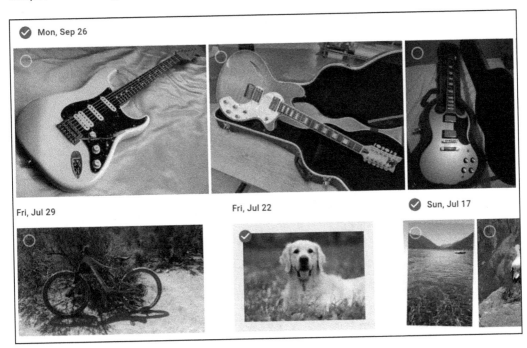

Figure 2.7

This is because Photos read the date information from the file itself rather than using the date it was uploaded. If you upload a photo with no date information (also known as metadata), it will use the date you uploaded the picture.

Fortunately, it's very easy to change the date and location information for a particular photograph. To do so, select the photo by checking the circle at the top left of the picture and then choose either *Edit date & time* or *Edit location* depending on what you want to do.

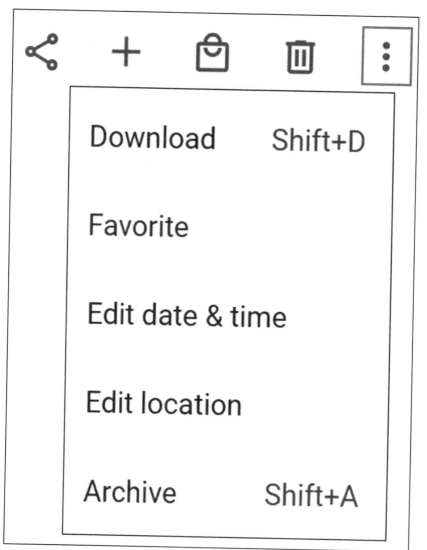

Figure 2.8

If you choose to edit the date and time, Photos will show you what it is using for its current date and time and then you can change it however you see fit. You can also choose a different time zone if needed.

Figure 2.9

If you choose to edit the location, you can type in any information you like here, even if the photo didn't have any location information to begin with.

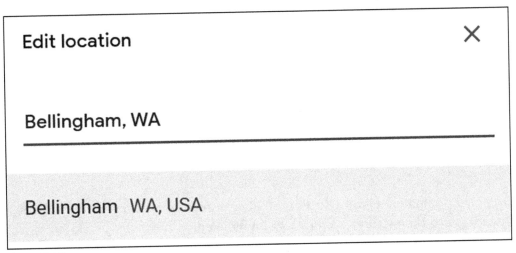

Figure 2.10

Now that I have changed the date of my photo to today's date, it shows up at the top of my list in the main photos area.

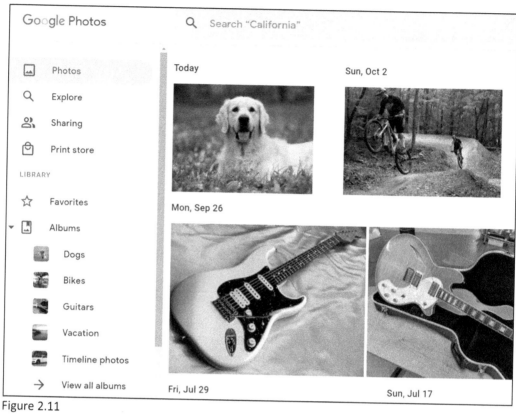

Figure 2.11

Searching for Photos

If you find that you have a lot of pictures in your Photos account, you may need to use the search feature to find your photos rather than scroll up and down the photos page or go through all of your albums to find any photo you are looking for.

When you upload a picture to Photos, it will analyze it and then add its own labels\tags to the pictures so they can be indexed with those tags. So if I search for **trails**, Photos found pictures of trails as well as bikes on trails.

Figure 2.12

If I search for **bikes**, Photos only shows pictures with bikes in them. As you can see in figure 2.13, it also shows a picture of a guitar so there must have been something about it that triggered Photos to show it in the search results. This is an example of the search feature not being perfect, but it does do a really good job most of the time.

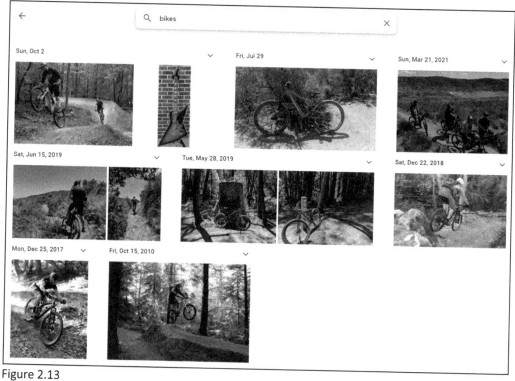

Figure 2.13

You can also search your photos using other methods such as location, date, file type and even combine these terms such as **lake 2022**.

Uploading Photos From Your Phone

Since most people use their smartphones for their cameras, it makes sense that you would want to be able to upload your files to your Photos account directly from your phone.

As I mentioned before, if you are using an Android based smartphone, there is a good chance that your photos are already being uploaded to your Photos account automatically. But if you don't want every photo going to your Photos account, you can turn off the backup feature as you saw in chapter 2.

If you turn off the backup feature, you will need to manually upload any photos (and videos) that you want to have stored in your Photos account. I prefer to do this rather than go through my Photos account and then have to delete pictures that I don't want to be kept there.

To upload a photo to your Google Photos account, you can select the photo or photos and then use the share option like you would to attach it to an email or text message. Then you can choose *Photos Upload* from the available apps on your phone.

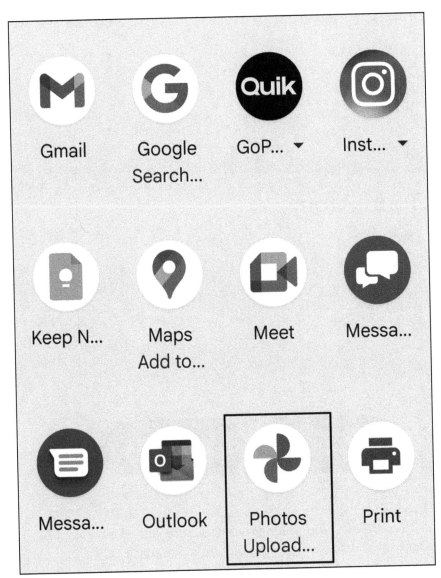

Figure 2.14

Then you can select the Google account that you use for your photos if you have more than one.

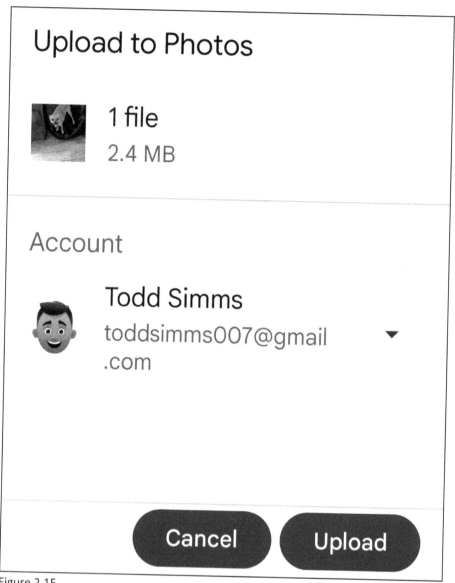

Figure 2.15

After the upload is complete, you will see your picture added to your Photos account with the date that was stored in the picture's metadata.

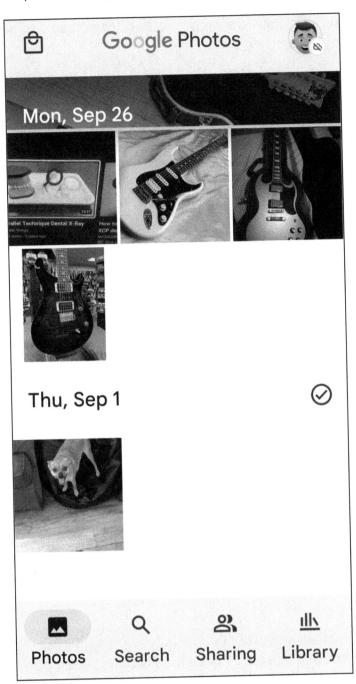

Figure 2.16

Creating Albums

Once you start accumulating a lot of pictures in your Photos account, you will come to realize that it gets harder to find the pictures you are looking for and you spend more time scrolling up and down the Photos website page than you do viewing your pictures.

This is where creating photo albums can save you time and also allow you to group your memories together in one place so you can see all of the pictures from a specific event or category.

To view your albums, simply click on the Albums section on the left side of the Photos interface. If you don't have any albums, this section will be blank, and you will have a button that you can click on to create an album. You will also have a create button option at the top of the screen.

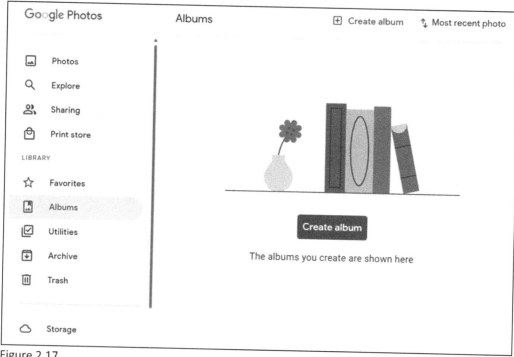

Figure 2.17

For my demo Photos account, I have several albums already in place and I can see them displayed with their name and number of pictures in each one listed below their preview image. I can then click on any of the albums to see what photos are part of that album.

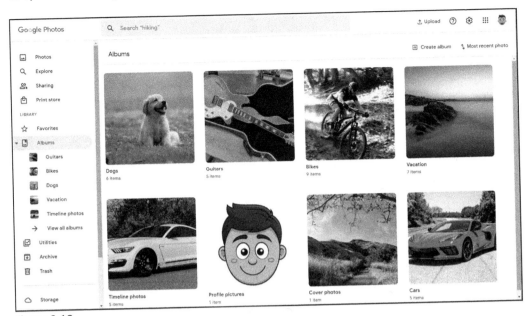

Figure 2.18

If I were to click on the three vertical dots at the top of each album preview image, I can then do things such as rename the album, share it (discussed in chapter 4), or delete the album. Deleting the album does not delete the pictures from your account and you will still be able to find them in your main Photos area.

Figure 2.19

If I wanted to use a different picture for the album cover, I can go into the album, open the photo I want to use for the cover and click on the three vertical dots in the upper right hand corner. Then from the drop down list, I would choose *use as album cover*. Figure 2.21 shows my albums section with my new dog album cover.

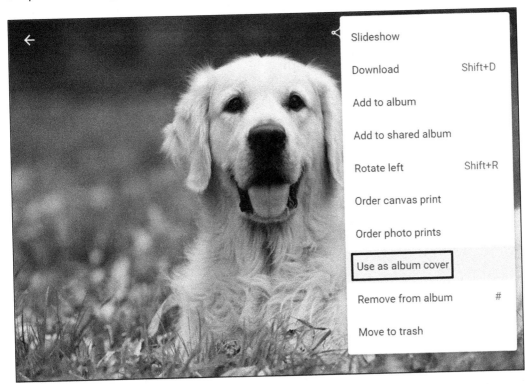

Figure 2.20

Figure 2.21

To create an album, all you need to do is click on *Create album* and then you will be prompted to give your new album a name. You will also have a choice between creating an auto-updating album or just a regular album.

Figure 2.22

If you choose the auto-updating album, Photos will ask you to choose some existing photos to base its updating criteria on. Then when you upload new pictures, Photos will look at them and if they match the people or pets, you chose when creating the album, it will add these new pictures to this album. Of course you will have to rely on Google being able to recognize your friends, family or pets so don't expect it to work perfectly.

I will choose the *Select photos* option to create a standard album and place my Hawaii vacation photos in this album. I will first name the album Hawaii Vacation. After clicking on the Select photos button, I will be brought to my main photos page where I can choose any existing pictures that I have in my Photos account. Since I don't have my Hawaii photos here, I will need to choose the *Select from computer* option.

Figure 2.23

I will then be able to select one or more pictures from my computer to upload to Photos. I can hold down the *Ctrl* key on my keyboard while selecting which photos I want to add rather than having to do them one at a time. I can also use the Ctrl-A keyboard shortcut to select all the photos in a particular folder. Once I have my pictures selected, I will click on the *Open* button.

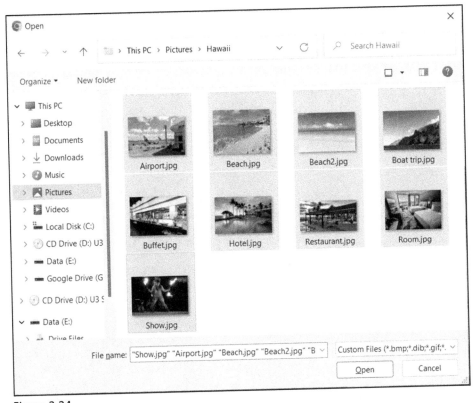

Figure 2.24

Now I have my new album created with all of the pictures I just uploaded.

Figure 2.25

Now when I go back to my main Photos section, I will see my new Hawaii pictures there along with all of my other pictures that were there previously (figure 2.26).

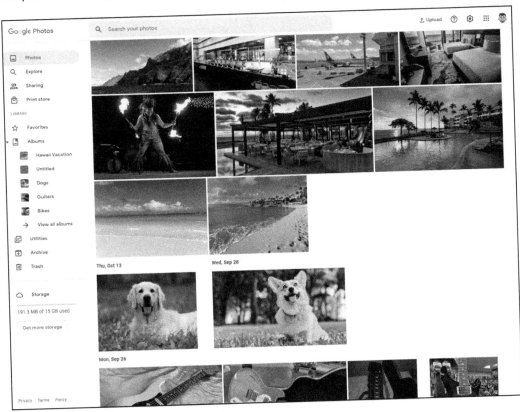

Figure 2.26

Editing Albums

Once you have a photo album created, you can then edit it so it looks the way you want it to. When you are in an album, you can click on the three vertical dots at the upper right hand of the screen and choose the *Edit album* option. You will also see additional choices such as running a slideshow of the images in that album as well as an option to download all the photos from that album to your computer.

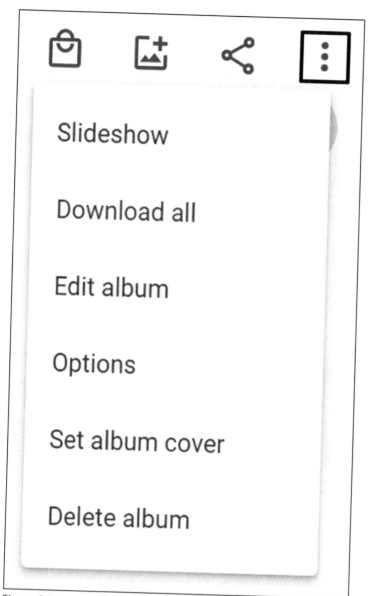

Figure 2.27

Once you are in the edit section, you will be able to click on any photo and drag it to a new location so you can change the order of the pictures in your album. If you want to delete a photo, you can select it and then click on the X at the upper left corner to remove it from the album. This will not delete the photo itself, but simply remove it from the album you are working in. You can also select multiple photos using the *Ctrl* or *Shift* keys on your keyboard and rearrange or remove them if needed.

Figure 2.28

You can also click on the name of the album and change it from here. Once you are finished with your changes, you will need to click on the checkmark next to *Edit album* at the upper left.

The *Options* choice that can be accessed from the same drop down menu can be used to configure your album to use the auto-updating feature that you can select when you first create the album. There are also some sharing options here, but I will be discussing sharing in chapter 4.

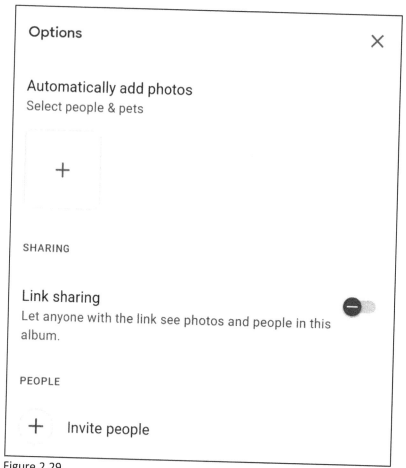

Figure 2.29

Favorites

If you commonly use a web browser on your computer to visit websites, you most likely have some favorites or bookmarks that you have created to make these commonly used websites easier to access the next time you need to go to them.

The favorites label in Photos works the same way by letting you mark your favorite pictures so you can find them easier since you most likely will be viewing them more often than other photos.

To mark a photo as a favorite, all you need to do is click on the star icon above the picture when viewing it as seen in figure 2.30.

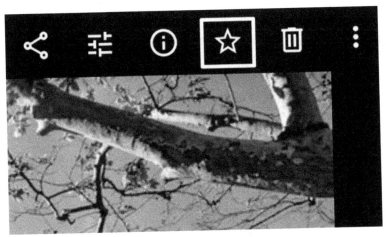

Figure 2.30

Then you will be able to go to your favorite section on the left above your listing of albums. Once you are there, you will only see photos that you have marked as a favorite. You will also notice that these favorites are marked with a star in the lower left corner even when viewing them in the main Pictures area as seen in figure 2.31.

Figure 2.31

To remove a photo from your favorites, simply select it and click on the three vertical dots in the upper left corner and then choose *Remove from Favorites*. This will only remove it from the favorites section and not delete the photo itself or remove it from any albums.

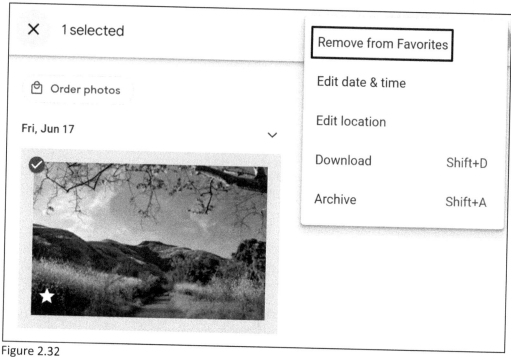

Figure 2.32

Explore Options

The Explore section is where you can go to see your photos and videos organized into categories based on what the Photos app thinks they are comprised of. As you can see in figure 2.33, Photos grouped my pictures into categories such as bikes and cars based on what it saw in the photos themselves. As you add more pictures to your Photos app, it will continue to build upon this content based on what the pictures contain.

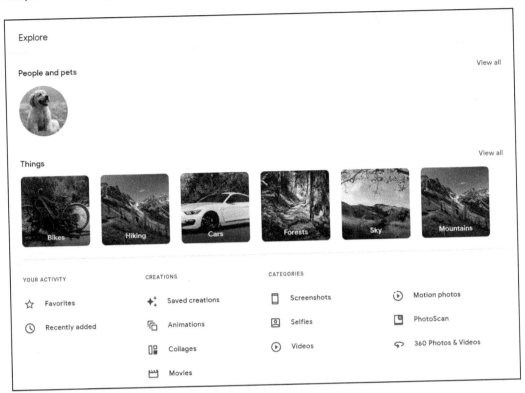

Figure 2.33

Assuming Photos has categorized your pictures and videos correctly, you can then click on any one of the sections to see the content that is related to that category. Once you create some animations, collages or movies, they will show up in the Creations section. I will be discussing these items in chapter 5.

Editing Photos
One of the best things about digital photos compared to printed photos is that you have the ability to edit them to either improve the way they look or add your own artistic flair to them.

There are many photo editing applications that you can use on your pictures and of course some work better than others. You most likely have a photo viewing program on your computer such as the Windows Photos app or the Preview app for Mac users which usually include some type of editing capabilities. And of course there are dedicated photo editing programs that you can buy if you really want to create some professional looking results.

> *If you want to learn how to use the inexpensive yet powerful Adobe Photoshop Elements, then check out my book titled **Photoshop Elements Made Easy**.*
> *https://www.amazon.com/dp/1688736352*

The Photos website allows you the option to edit your photos right from the website itself. To get to the editor section, open the photo you want to edit and click on the edit icon in the toolbar.

Figure 2.34

You will have several methods that you can use to enhance or edit your pictures. Figure 2.35 shows the enhancement section where you can choose a filter to apply to your photo to give it a custom look. Once you choose your filter, you can use the slider to adjust how it is applied to your photo. If you don't like what you see, you can then click on *Undo edits*. The *Click & hold to compare* option will let you toggle between the filter and the original so you can see the difference.

Once you like the way it looks, simply click on the *Done* button to have the filter applied to your photo. If you want to save your edits as a new file and leave the original intact, you can click on the three vertical dots next to the Done option and then choose *Save copy* to have a new file created with the changes.

Figure 2.35

The next section will let you change the brightness and adjust the colors. The *Pop* setting highlights shadows and gives your photo more of an artistic look.

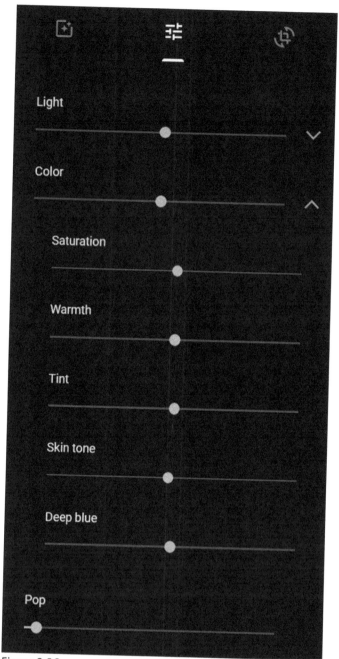

Figure 2.36

The last section will allow you to crop and rotate your picture as needed. You can also change the aspect ratio using one of the predefined settings. You can also change your picture from landscape to portrait but just keep in mind that some of it will be cropped out.

Figure 2.37

Chapter 3 – Storage

As you probably know, photos take up space on the hard drive in your computer and that means they also take up space on the hard drives that Google uses to store your photos in the cloud. I mentioned that the free Google accounts come with 15 GB of storage and that storage is used for other Google apps such as Drive and Gmail, so you need to be aware of how much space you are using.

Storage Settings
Photos has a storage section at the bottom left of the screen that you can click on to get detailed information about what types of files are using your storage as well as what Google apps these files are being used with. You can also use the following website address to get to these settings.
https://photos.google.com/quotamanagement

Figure 3.1 shows that this account has not used much of its total storage and 20 MB (megabytes) used towards photos and videos. It also shows that the account has only used 147 MB out of the total 15 GB available.

It's a good idea to have a basic understanding of how the conversions between all the various file sizes work. Besides MB and GB we also have TB, kB, bytes and so on. You can find online conversion calculators to help you if needed.

Under *Review and delete* you would be shown any files that are unusually large so you can decide if they are worth keeping or maybe even moving somewhere else to free up space in your account.

More than 4 years of storage left

Personal estimate based on how often you back up content to your Google Account

● Google Photos (20.1 MB) ● Drive, Gmail, and more (127.3 MB)   147.4 MB of 15 GB used

> (1) **Get more storage**
> With a Google One plan. Storage is shared across Photos, Drive, and Gmail
>
> Get started

Review and delete

🖼 Large photos & videos   ~0 MB

⚏ Blurry photos   ~0 MB

⚏ Other apps   ~0 MB

▢ Screenshots   ~0 MB

⊙ Unsupported videos

Recover storage

🖼 Convert existing photos & videos to Storage saver   Learn more

Other suggestions

① Clean up Gmail & Drive   Review items
   Review and delete large attachments, files, and items with Google One

⑦ Find out more about how storage works   Learn more

Figure 3.1

Under *Other suggestions* and then *Clean up Gmail & Drive* you can click on *Review items* to get some suggestions on how you can get some space back (figure 3.2).

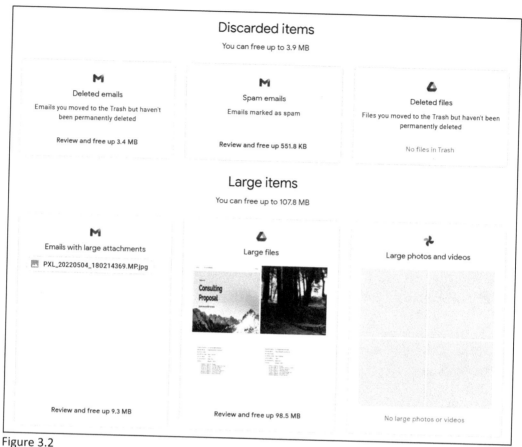

Figure 3.2

If you find that you are a big fan of Google Photos and other Google apps and want to get more storage space, you can consider purchasing one of the subscription plans that were discussed in chapter 1.

Archiving Photos

At some point, you will probably find that you have some photos that you don't really look at or share with others and they are just getting in the way and making your main Photos section look a bit crowded. Fortunately, you can remove them from the main Photos area and place them in your archive rather than delete them just in case you want to view them later.

To archive a photo or photos, you will need to select them from the main Photos area (not from an album) and then you can click on the three vertical dots at the upper right corner and then choose *Archive*.

Figure 3.3

You will then see a message letting you know your photos were archived and you can either click on *Done* or *Go to Archive* to see your newly archived pictures (figure 3.5).

Figure 3.4

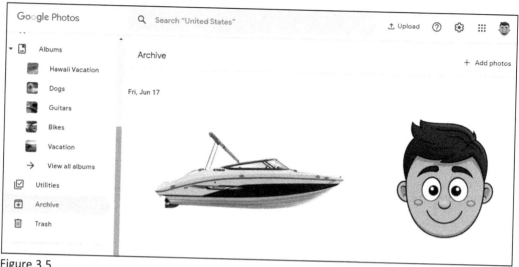

Figure 3.5

If you choose to archive a photo that is in an album, it will stay in the album but be removed from the main Photos area.

To remove a photo from the Archive section and place it back in the main Photos area, you can select one or more from your Archive, click the three vertical dots and then choose *Unarchive*.

Trash

Just like you can with photos on your computer, you can delete any pictures or movies from Google Photos that you do not want to be stored online any longer. Once you delete a photo, it will be moved to your trash as well as removed from any albums it was part of.

You can go to the Trash section within Photos to view any pictures or videos you have recently deleted (figure 3.6). One thing you will notice when you go there is that there will be a message saying *Items will be permanently deleted after 60 days from Trash*. This means that once you delete a photo, it will stay in your trash for 60 days and then you will not be able to recover it.

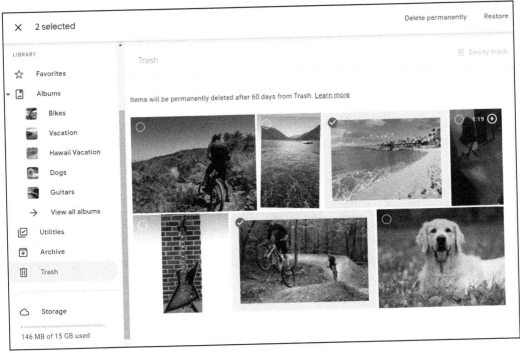

Figure 3.6

If you want to remove an item from the trash before the 60 days is up, you can select it and then click on *Delete permanently*. Or you can click on *Empty trash* to have everything in your Trash removed for good.

To restore one or more items, simply check each one you want to restore and then click on the *Restore* link at the top of the page. The photos will then be placed back in their original location as well as be placed back in any albums they were a part of.

Chapter 4 – Sharing Your Photos

One of the best features of cloud based storage is the ability to share your files with others and participate in online collaboration without needing to email files back and forth and hope that you are working with the latest version. Just like most of the other Google applications, Photos will let you share your pictures, videos and albums with other people, so you don't have to worry about trying to attach 50 vacation pictures to one email and hope that it goes through!

Sharing Photos and Videos

Google Photos makes it easy to share your pictures with others, as long as they have a Google account. And by Google account, I don't mean a Gmail address but rather any email address associated with a Google account. For those who don't have Google accounts, you can use links which I will be discussing later in the chapter.

To share a photo or photos, simply select them from either your main Photos section or from an album and then click on the share icon as seen in figure 4.1.

Figure 4.1

Next, you can either type in the person's email address or choose them from your Google contacts. If you want to share the photos with multiple people, you can click on *New group* and select more than one email address to add to the recipient list.

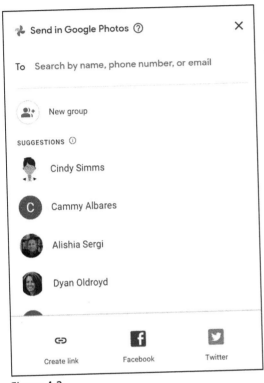

Figure 4.2

Once you have your recipient(s) chosen, you can send a personal message with the shared photos. If you need to add additional photos, you can click the + icon to the left of the send button.

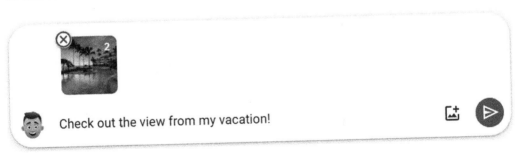

Figure 4.3

Once you have shared your photos, they will be shown in the *Sharing* section in your Photos account, and it will also tell you who you have shared them with. If you click on the three vertical dots (More options), you can then choose *Leave* which will remove the photos and any comments from being shared.

Figure 4.4

The person who you shared the photos with will get an email with your message and it will have a button that they can click on to view your shared photos.

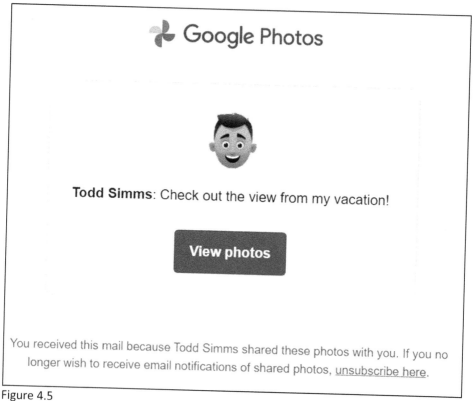

Figure 4.5

Then they will also be able to add comments to your photos which you will be able to see. If they click on *Save*, the pictures will be added to their Photos account as well. If you stop sharing on your end but the other person has already saved your photos to their account, they will still have their own copy of the photos.

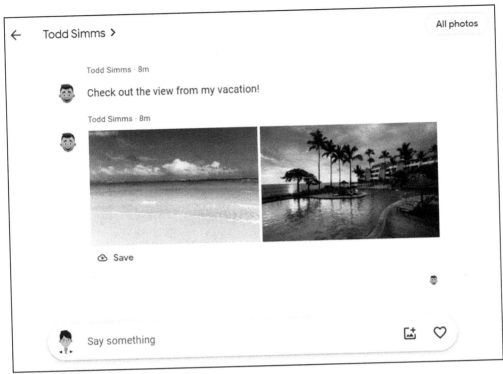

Figure 4.6

If you try and share photos or videos with an email address that is not associated with a Google account, you will get a message similar to the one shown in figure 4.7. But as I mentioned previously, you can use shared links for this type of situation.

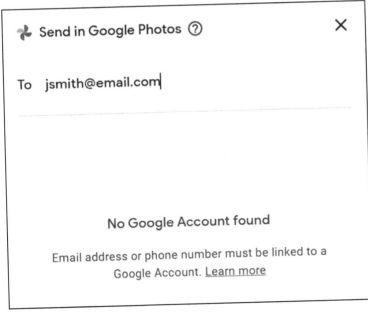

Figure 4.7

Sharing Albums

If you want to share an entire album rather than a picture or two, you can easily do so, and it works in a similar fashion to sharing photos. While in the album you want to share, click on the same share icon at the upper right and you will be presented with a similar list of contacts where you can choose an existing contact or type in an email address.

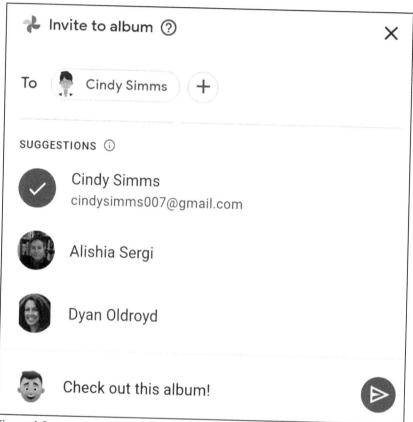

Figure 4.8

When the recipient gets your invitation, they can click on the button that says *View album* to be taken to your shared album.

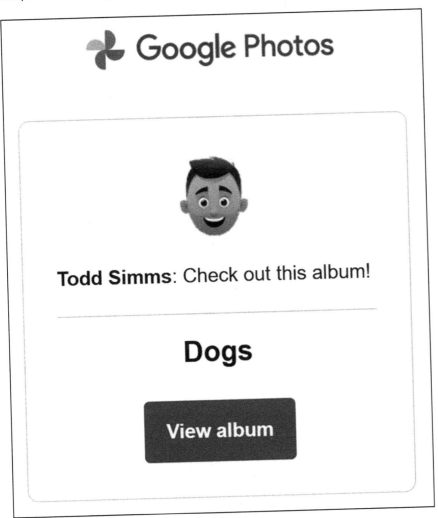

Figure 4.9

Then the people you shared the album with will be able to see your photos and videos and be able to make comments on the album that you will be able to see and respond to.

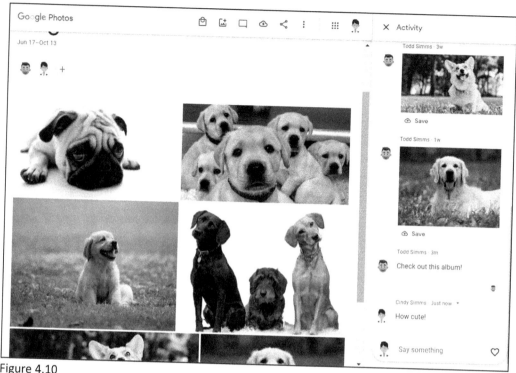

Figure 4.10

They will also be able to add their own photos to your album as well as share it with other people.

When someone adds their own photo to your album, it will show their name at the bottom as well as show your name for your own photos.

Figure 4.11

You can change some of these settings by clicking on the three vertical dots in the upper right corner and choosing *Options*. Under the *Sharing* settings, you can enable or disable sharing photo locations, and allow others to add their own photos, comments and share links.

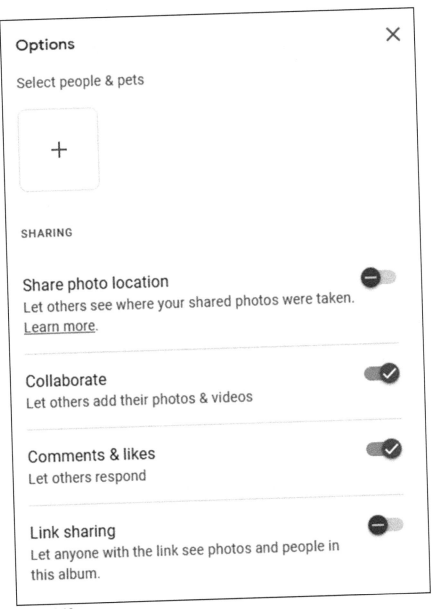

Figure 4.12

To remove a person from your shared album, you can click on their name under the album name and then click the three vertical dots and choose *Remove person*.

Figure 4.13

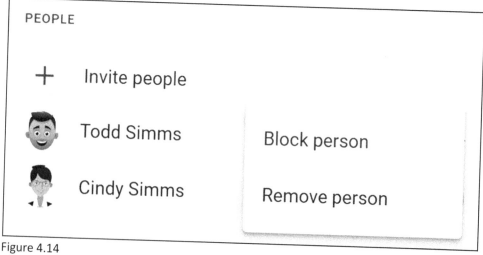

Figure 4.14

Creating Shared Links

If you would like to share your photos or an album with people and are not sure if they have a Google account, you can simply create a link to that photo or album and then copy and paste it into an email and send it off to whoever you would like to give access to.

When you choose the share option, there will be a choice at the bottom that says *Create link* (figure 4.15).

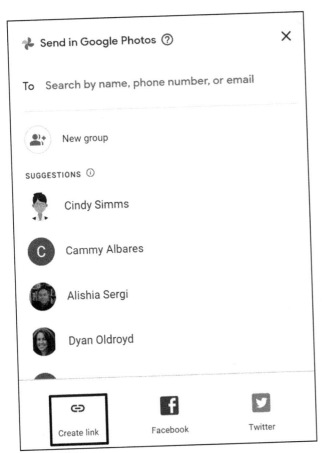

Figure 4.15

When you click on this you will be told that anyone with the link will be able to view your photos. If you agree with that then you can click the *Create link* button.

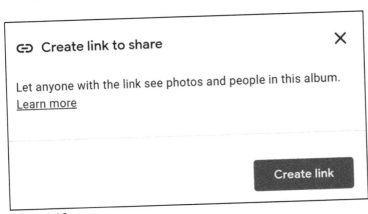

Figure 4.16

Now you can click on the *Copy* button to copy the link and then you can paste it into an email or chat etc. and send it to the people who you want to see your photos.

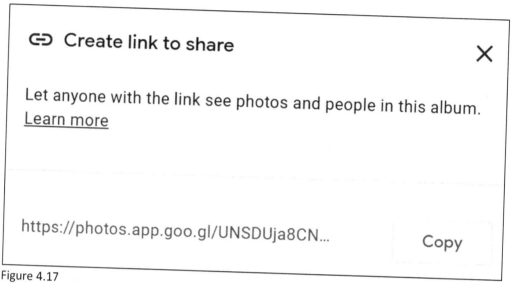

Figure 4.17

If someone opens the link and doesn't have a Google account or is not signed into their Google account, they will not be able to do things such as save pictures, send chat messages or reshare your album without signing in with a Google account first.

Partner Sharing
If you have someone that you always share your photos with then you might want to check out the Partner Sharing feature of Google Photos. Rather than texting or emailing them new pictures or even sharing them one at a time via Photos, you can configure your account to always share your pictures with them.

Partner Sharing works by choosing a person or people and then deciding which types of photos and from what date you want to share with them. Then as you add new pictures that meet the Partner Sharing criteria to your account, they will automatically be shared with the people you have chosen.

If you go to the Sharing section of Photos, you will see your current shared photos and albums and you will also have an option to set up Partner Sharing.

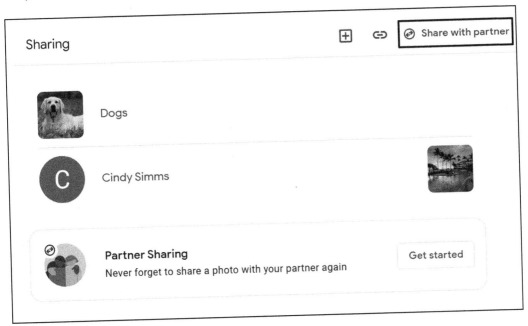

Figure 4.18

Once you start the process you will be asked what types of photos to share and how far you want to go back date wise based on the dates of your pictures. You can choose either all photos or photos of certain people assuming the Photos app has already taken an inventory of people in your pictures based on their faces. Just remember, this process isn't perfect so you might end up sharing photos of people you don't want to share.

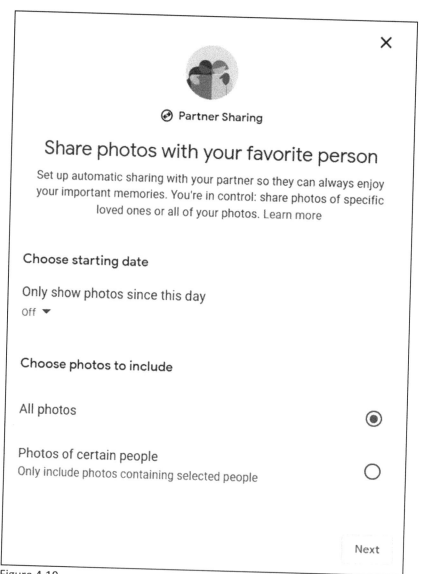

Figure 4.19

I will choose the *All photos* option and set my start date to be January 1st, 2020.

Figure 4.20

After I click the *Next* button, I will be prompted to choose who I want to set up this new partner share with.

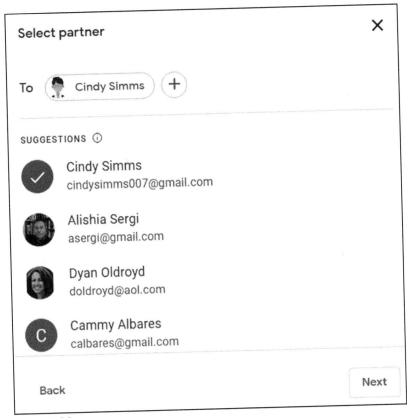

Figure 4.21

Next, I will be shown a summary screen and if everything looks good, I can click on the *Send invitation* button.

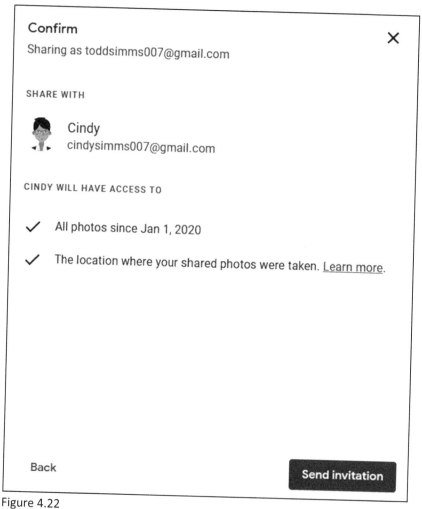

Figure 4.22

Now when I go back to my Sharing section, I will see the new Partner Share along with my other shared photos and albums.

Figure 4.23

When the invitee gets the email about my Partner Share, they can click on the button that says *View invite*. Once again, they will need to have a Google account to use this feature.

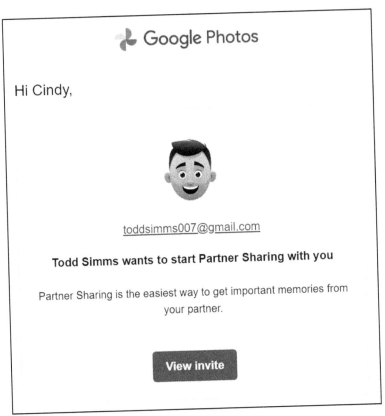

Figure 4.24

They will then be asked to accept the invitation by clicking the *Accept* button.

Figure 4.25

Next, they will be asked if they want to set up a Partner Share with you and share some of their own photos. This is optional and they can click on the *Not now* button if they don't want to set this up.

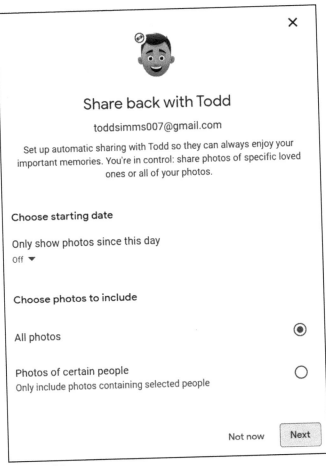

Figure 4.26

Now when the invitee goes into their Share section, they will see your Partner Share along with their other shared items. Now every time you upload a picture that meets the Partner Share criteria, it will be automatically shared with them.

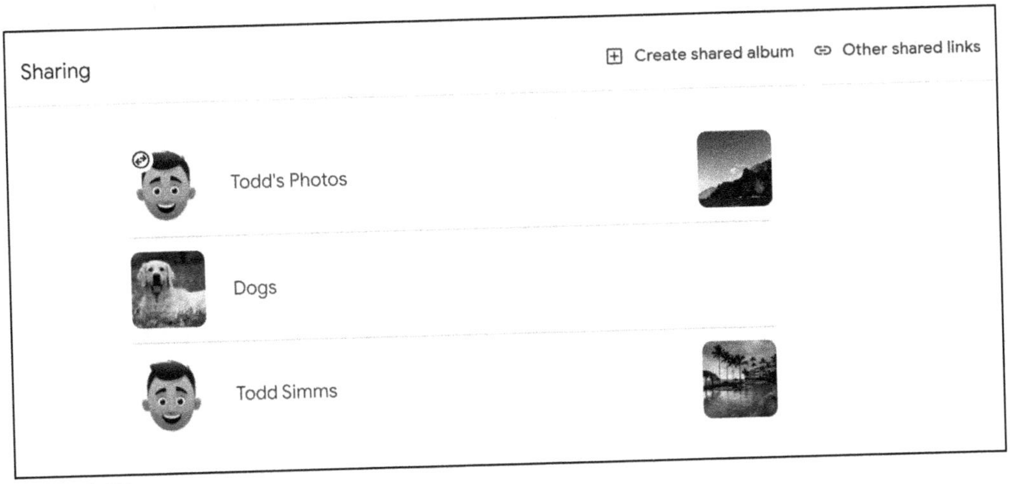

Sharing

⊞ Create shared album   ⊖ Other shared links

Todd's Photos

Dogs

Todd Simms

Figure 4.27

Chapter 5 – Utilities

Google Photos is not just all about storing and sharing your pictures. It also comes with some utilities you can use to do things such as create movies, animations and collages from your photos. In this chapter, I will show you how to use these extra features so you can have a little fun with your photos.

Movies

Besides uploading pictures to your Photos account, you can also upload videos as well. But if you want to create a movie from your pictures then you can try out the *Movie* option under the *Utilities* section.

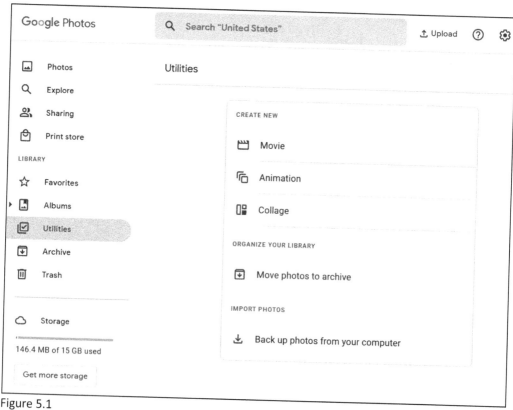

Figure 5.1

Once you start your movie, you can choose from one of the built in templates or create your own. There is a catch if you want to use one of the templates though. You will need to have photos of the same person or pet etc. because it will want to use the same dog or child for the video for example.

Figure 5.2

So if I choose the *Doggie Movie* option, it will tell me that it works best if you have a lot of photos of a particular dog, not dogs in general.

Figure 5.3

When I click the *Get Started* button, I will be shown any pictures that Photos has tagged as being dogs. But in this case since they are all different dogs, I can only choose one and then I am told that it is unable to create the movie because there are not enough photos for the movie (figure 5.4).

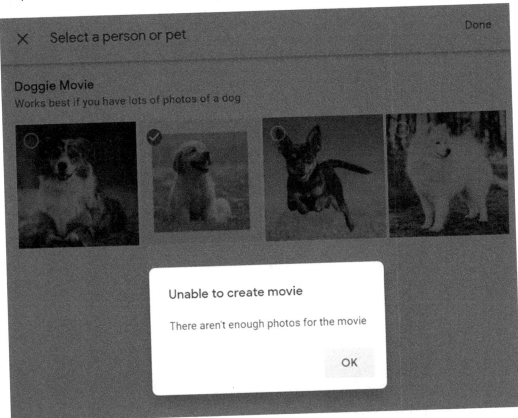

Figure 5.4

 *Google Photos is pretty hit or miss when it comes to tagging faces and pets so don't count on it to be a perfect solution to keep your family members or pets organized.*

To get around this and make a movie using all of my dog pictures, I will go back and choose the *New movie* option. I will then manually select all of the different dog pictures from my photos up to a maximum of 50 pictures and then click on *Create*.

I will then be taken to the movie editor (figure 5.5) where I can do things such as click on the three vertical dots next to a picture insert additional photos, duplicate a photo or remove it. I can also drag the slider next to each picture to determine how long that picture plays in the movie. I can also drag and drop the photo clips to rearrange the order they play in the movie.

As you can see, the movie is set to play in portrait mode which is cutting off the left and right sides of some of my pictures so I can either live with that or change it to landscape mode by clicking the icon next to the musical instrument note which is used to add music to your video.

Figure 5.5

If you click on the music option, you will have several categories of music with multiple songs in each category to choose from (figure 5.6).

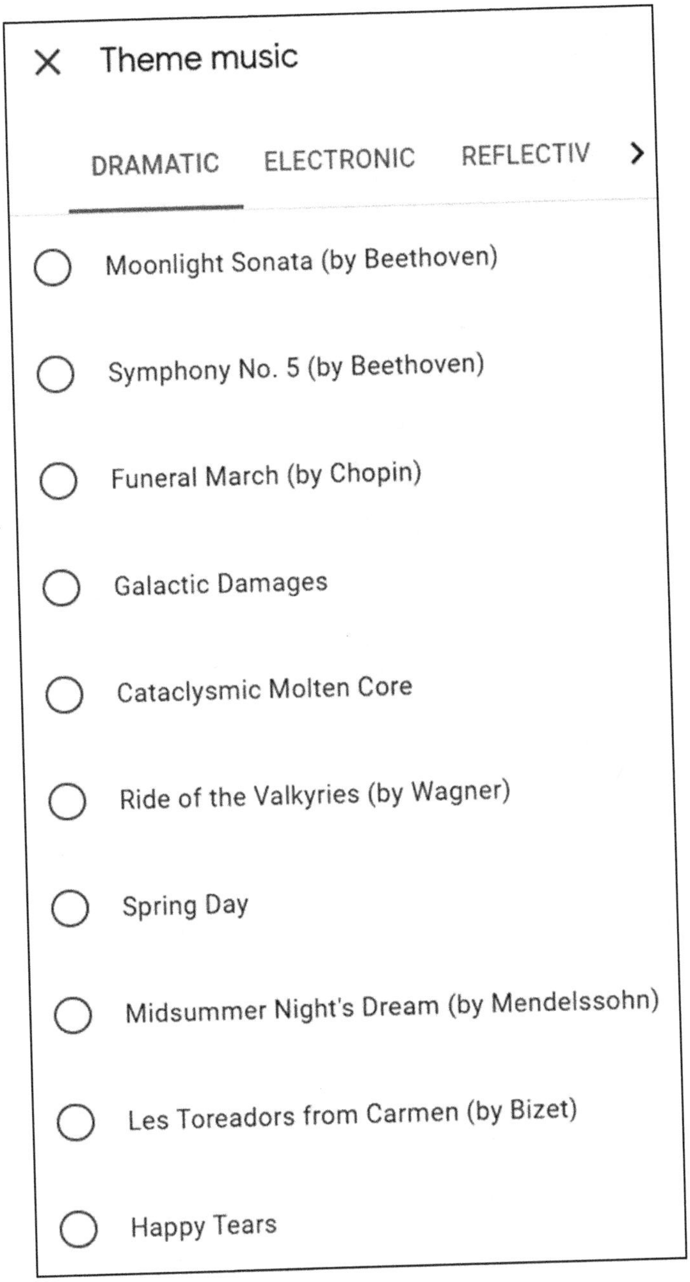

Figure 5.6

At any time during the editing process, you can click the play button in the middle of the movie preview to see how your movie will look when it's ready. Once everything is looking the way you like, you can click on *Save* to have your new movie created. The movie creating process will take several minutes and the more photos you have added, the longer it will take.

You will then be shown your movie where you can add a description, change the date and also add a location if needed. Plus you will also have the usual share, favorite and delete options like you are used to seeing for your photos.

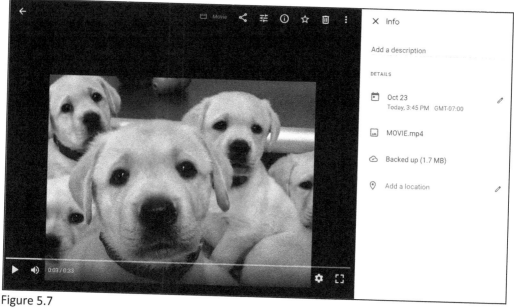

Figure 5.7

If you click on the three vertical dots next to the delete trash can icon, you will have some additional options such as adding it to an album or downloading the movie to your computer. I will add my movie to my Dogs album and then it will show up there with my photos and I can play it simply by clicking on it. If I want to edit the video, I can do so after I open it by clicking on the Edit icon like you would do for photos.

Animations

Another thing you can do in Photos is create an animated slideshow from any photos you wish to use. This process simply makes an animated GIF image file out of your photos that you can also share or download to your computer.

To start the process, choose anywhere from 2 to 50 photos from your account and click on *Create*.

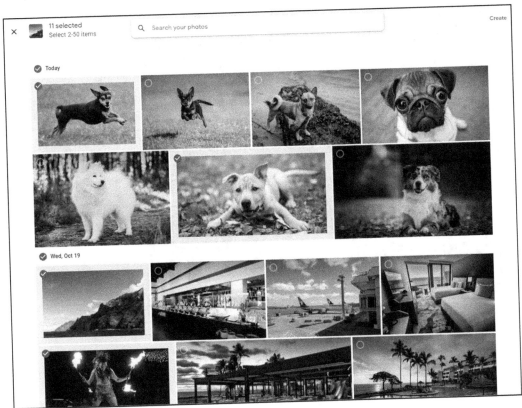

Figure 5.8

It will then create the animated slideshow and once again you can add a description, change the date or add a location. You can also add the slideshow to an album or share it as needed.

Figure 5.9

You will be able to find your animation in the Photos section as well as in any albums you added it to.

Collages

Photos allows you to choose up to 9 pictures to add to a photo collage that you can save to your account or even share and print. Once you choose the Collage option, you will then select the photos you wish to use just like we saw for the animation feature.

Once you click on Create, you will then be able to edit your collage just like you could for the video and animation features.

Figure 5.10

One thing that you can do with collages that you can't with videos or animations is apply the same editing options that you saw for photos. You can add filters, edit the brightness and colors and also crop and rotate your collage.

Figure 5.11

Once you have created a movie, animation or collage, you will be able to spot them by the icon they have in the upper right hand corner when looking through your photos. Movies will have a movie clapperboard icon with the length of the video and animations and collages have a three star icon as seen in figure 5.12.

Figure 5.12

Locked Folder

If you are using the Google Photos app on an Android based smartphone, you will have an additional option called Locked Folder which you won't see on your PC or iPhone.

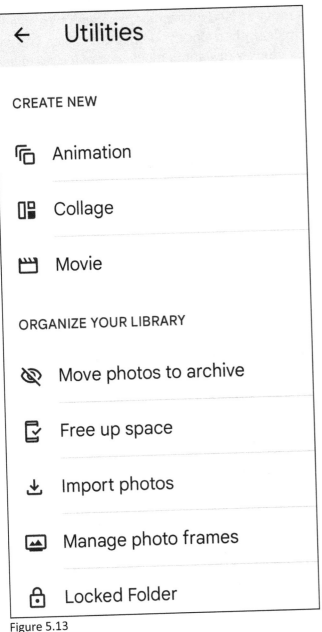

Figure 5.13

This special folder is used to store photos and videos that you want to have kept private, so they won't show up in searches, albums, and other apps on your device. They also won't be backed up or shared and if you uninstall the Photos app from your phone and get a new one, any items in this folder will be deleted. Of course you have the option to move them out of this locked folder in case you do want them available to other apps or backed up.

To use the Locked Folder, you will also need to have your phone configured with some sort of lock screen such as a pin or face recognition. You won't be able to take screenshots of your locked folder either. Once you open the utility, you will be able to choose which photos or videos you want to move to your locked folder.

Figure 5.14

Once they are moved to this folder, you will only be able to access them from here and will need to use your phone's security lock (PIN, password etc.) to access these photos and videos.

Once you are in the folder, you can select any items and then choose to have them removed from the locked folder.

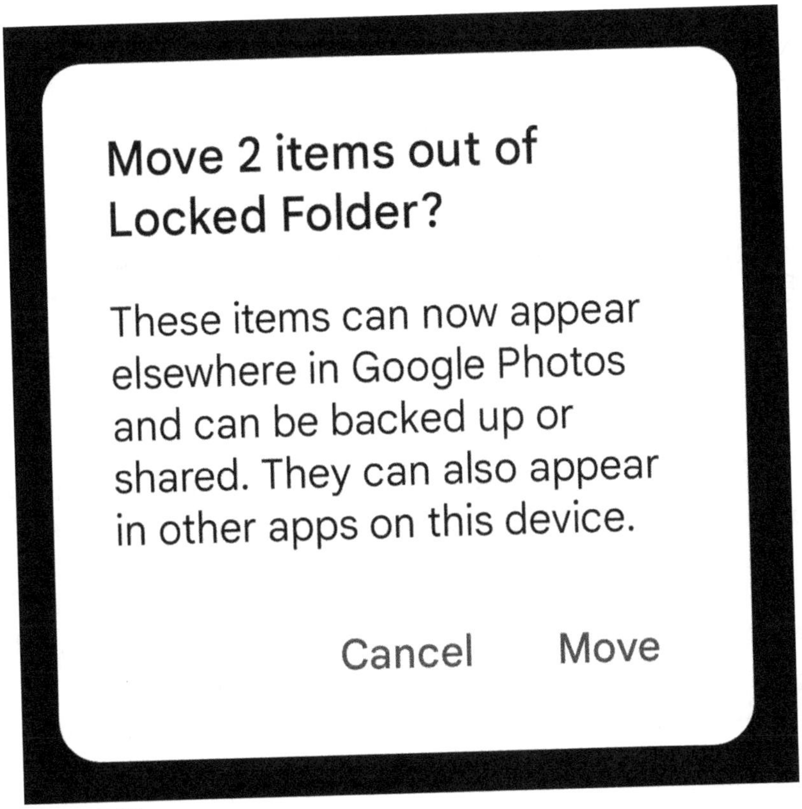

> # Move 2 items out of Locked Folder?
>
> These items can now appear elsewhere in Google Photos and can be backed up or shared. They can also appear in other apps on this device.
>
> Cancel   Move

Figure 5.15

Chapter 6 – Ordering Prints

If you are old enough to remember the days when you had to have film developed and printed to see your pictures, you might feel the need to reminisce about the fun you had waiting a week to be able to see your pictures and actually have some prints made.

Of course you can print your photos at home if you have a photo printer or even a good color laser or inkjet printer, but they won't look as good as if you had them printed professionally. There are many stores out there that can make prints from your digital files, and you can either take them in on a flash drive or CD or upload them to their website and then wait for the prints to arrive in the mail. But if you are a serious Google Photos user, then you can order prints right from your account to make things easier on yourself.

Types of Prints Available

Before you have your photos printed and shipped out to your home, you will first need to decide what types of prints you want to have created. Photos offers several options when it comes to the types of prints you can order.

When you go to the Print store section in Google Photos, you will see that you have several options as to what types of photo prints you can order (figure 6.1). It will also show you the starting prices and of course the prices will go up depending on how fancy you want to get!

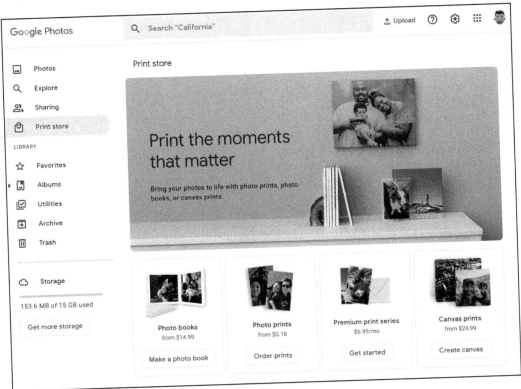

Figure 6.1

Here is a breakdown of the types of prints you can order.

- **Photo books** – You have the option to create a softcover or hardcover book with up to 245 items consisting of photos or collages. The softcover book will be cheaper than the hardcover version and the more photos you add, the more it will cost to print.

- **Photo prints** – If you want to order individual prints of specific photos, you can pick and choose which ones you want to print and their quantities. You can then choose store pickup or have them shipped to your house. Photos offers same day pickup and popular stores such as CVS, Walmart and Walgreens.

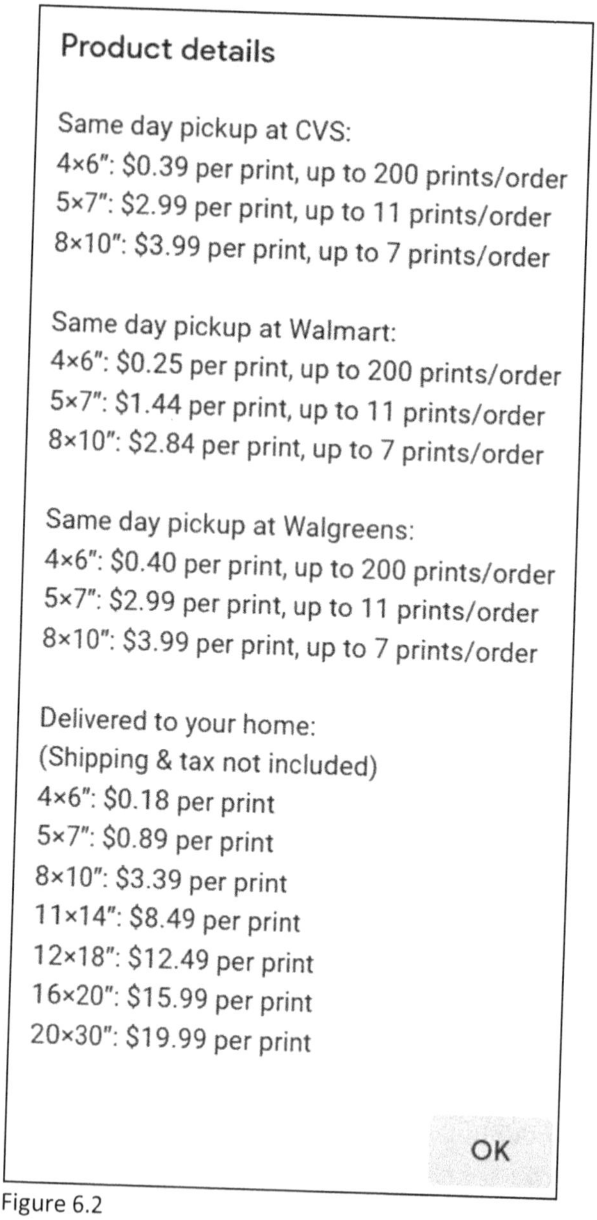

Product details

Same day pickup at CVS:
4×6": $0.39 per print, up to 200 prints/order
5×7": $2.99 per print, up to 11 prints/order
8×10": $3.99 per print, up to 7 prints/order

Same day pickup at Walmart:
4×6": $0.25 per print, up to 200 prints/order
5×7": $1.44 per print, up to 11 prints/order
8×10": $2.84 per print, up to 7 prints/order

Same day pickup at Walgreens:
4×6": $0.40 per print, up to 200 prints/order
5×7": $2.99 per print, up to 11 prints/order
8×10": $3.99 per print, up to 7 prints/order

Delivered to your home:
(Shipping & tax not included)
4×6": $0.18 per print
5×7": $0.89 per print
8×10": $3.39 per print
11×14": $8.49 per print
12×18": $12.49 per print
16×20": $15.99 per print
20×30": $19.99 per print

OK

Figure 6.2

- **Premium print series** – If you think you will want to print your photos on a regular basis, you can choose the Premium print series for $6.99\month for 10 high quality 4x6 glossy or matte photo prints of your choosing.

- **Canvas prints** – One fun thing you can do with your photos is to have them printed on a large canvas material, so it comes out more like a piece of artwork rather than a photo. You can edit your picture before you place your order and then choose the size you want to have it printed on.

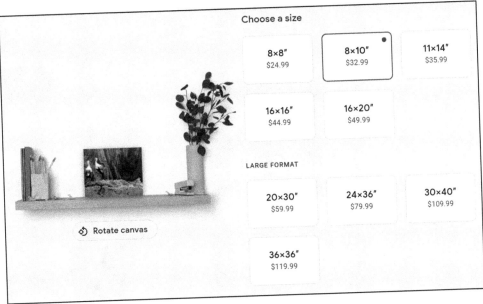

Figure 6.3

The Ordering Process

Once you decide which type of prints you want to buy, you can start your order. The process for making the order is a little different depending on what type of prints you choose but it shouldn't be too difficult to figure out.

Ordering a Photo Book

When ordering a photo book, you will be asked to select from 20 up to 245 pictures from your photo collection to start the process. If you do not add enough photos for the book, you will be notified that you need to add more to continue.

I have added my dog pictures plus some others to get to the 20 photo minimum. But now I can see that I have 13 warning messages at the top of the page. I can also see that there is a warning exclamation point on some of my photos indicating a problem (figure 6.4).

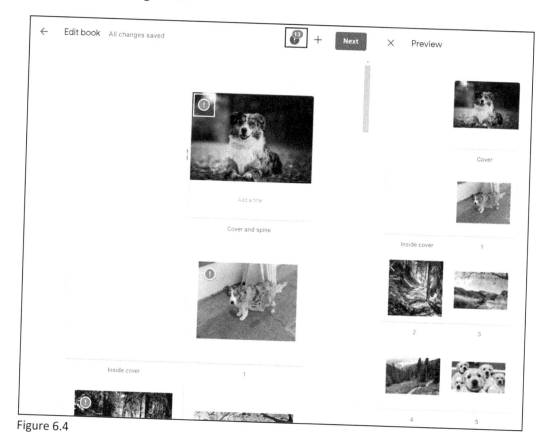

Figure 6.4

When I click on the warning message at the top of the page, I will get a listing of all the issues with my photo book in progress. As you can see in figure 6.5, I am missing a title for my book and have some photos that have too low of a resolution meaning the quality is not as good as it should be for printing.

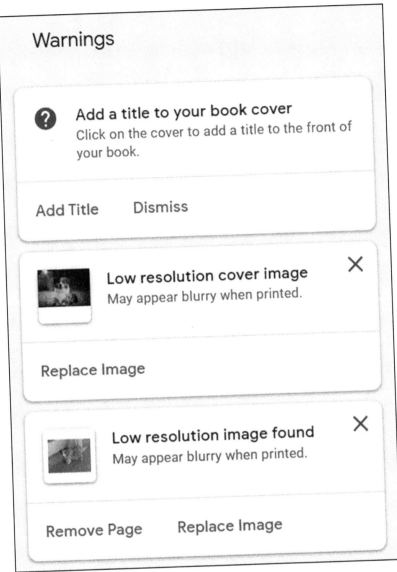

Figure 6.5

If I don't want to include the lower resolution images, I can click on *remove page* to not use that photo or *replace image* to use a different one. If I want to take my chances and keep the lower quality photos, I can just click on the X for each one I want to ignore. Once I have everything in place, I will click the *Next* button.

Next, I will need to decide if I want a softcover or hardcover book and then click the Select button.

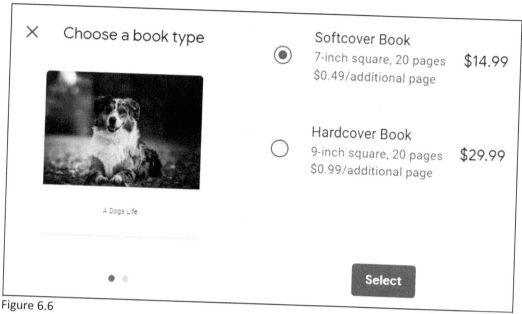

Figure 6.6

I will then be shown the price for my photo book and can choose how many books I want to have printed if I want more than just the one. Once I click the *Checkout* button, I will need to enter my shipping and payment information to complete my order.

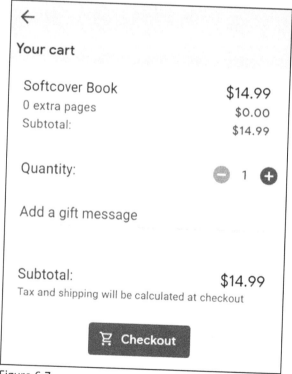

Figure 6.7

Ordering Photo Prints

The photo print ordering process starts the same as the photo book process but this time you can order up to 1200 prints. After I select the pictures I want to print and click the *Done* button, I will once again be shown any issues indicated by the red exclamation point on my photos.

Figure 6.8

Once again, I can replace any low resolution images or simply ignore them and have them printed anyway. At the bottom of each photo, you can change the default 4x6 size to one of the other options and also have the new size applied to all of the selected photos by checking the *Apply size to all prints* checkbox.

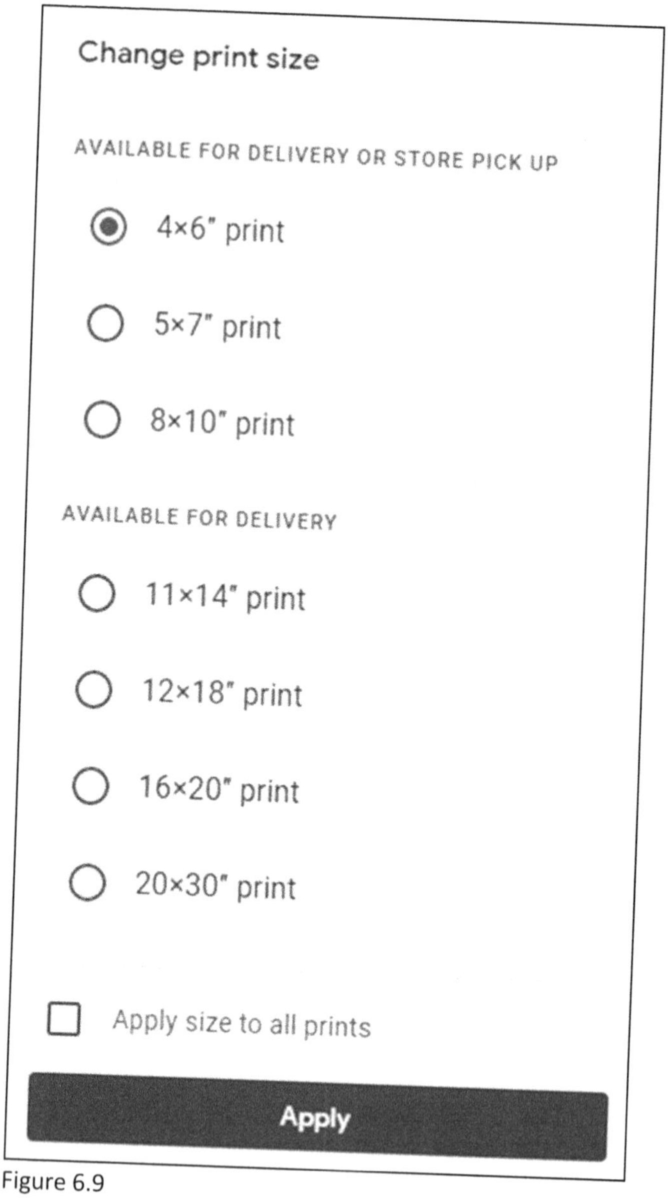

Figure 6.9

I can also crop or edit my photos just like I was able to do before and if I want more than one copy of a specific photo, I can change that from here as well.

Once I click the *Next* button, I will be asked if I want to have my photos delivered or if I want to pick them up at a local store along with the price for each option.

If I choose the *Ship my order* option, I will need to enter my shipping and payment information like I did for the photo book. If I want to pick them up at a local store, I can choose the *Store pickup* option and click on the *Next* button.

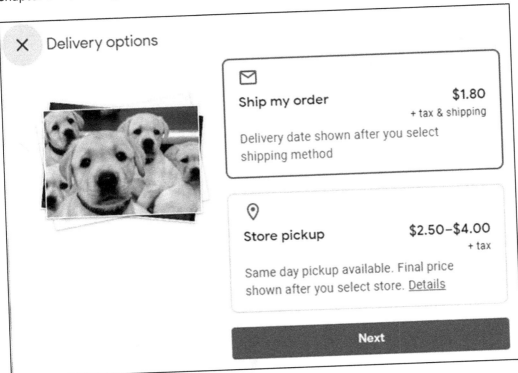

Figure 6.10

I can then either have my computer find local stores using any location information it has stored or I can type in a location and do a search of the surrounding area (figure 6.11).

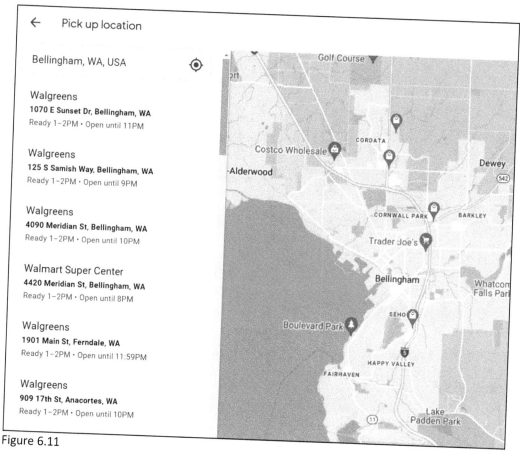

Figure 6.11

Once I choose the store I want to use, I can then complete my order and pick them up the same day unless you order them when the store is closed of course.

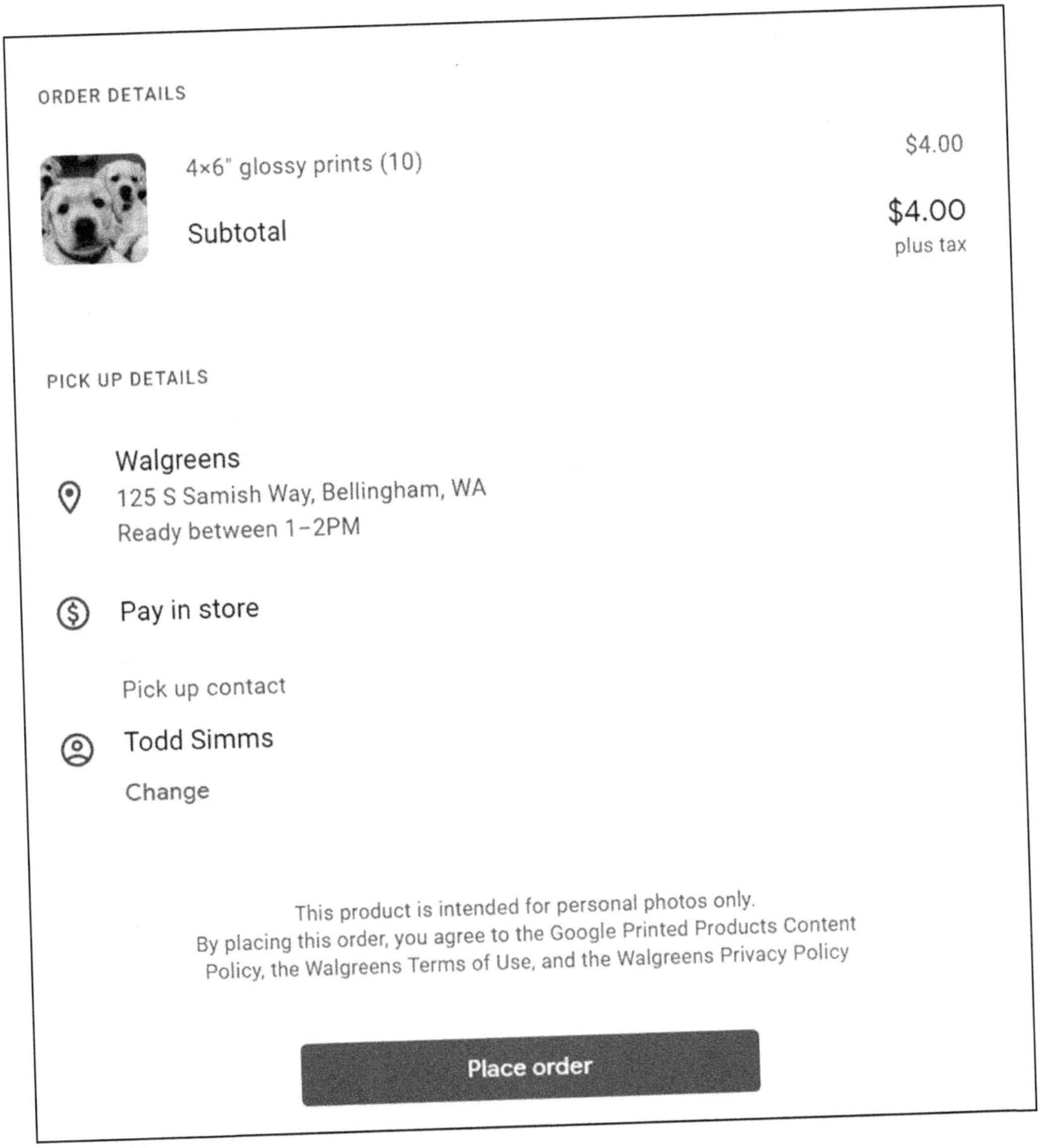

ORDER DETAILS

4×6" glossy prints (10) $4.00

Subtotal   **$4.00**
                                                                  plus tax

PICK UP DETAILS

Walgreens
125 S Samish Way, Bellingham, WA
Ready between 1–2PM

Pay in store

Pick up contact

Todd Simms

Change

This product is intended for personal photos only.
By placing this order, you agree to the Google Printed Products Content
Policy, the Walgreens Terms of Use, and the Walgreens Privacy Policy

Place order

Figure 6.12

Signing up for Premium Prints
If you want to have photos printed on a monthly basis you can sign up for Premium
Prints by clicking the *Get started* button.

If you have some people or pets tagged\recognized by Photos, you will be able to
select them from the next screen. If you don't want to use any of your tagged
photos, you can click on *Skip*.

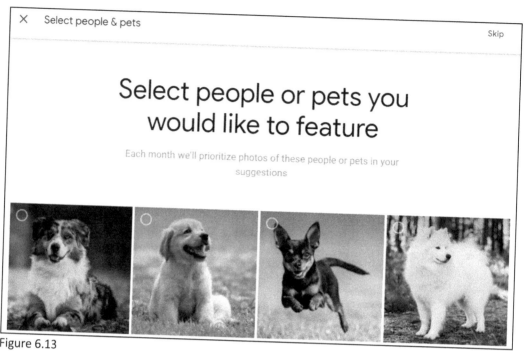

Figure 6.13

Next, you will need to choose your paper finish and print border options. You can also have the date printed on the back of the photo as well. If you enable the Show postcard option, your prints will have a postcard format printed on the back, so they are ready to put a stamp on and place in the mail.

Figure 6.14

Next, Photos will show you some photos that it thinks you might want to have printed. If you don't want to use these, you can click on *Replace* and you can also crop or edit them as needed.

Figure 6.15

After you confirm your selections, you will once again be brought to the shipping and payment page where you can complete your order.

Ordering Canvas Prints
If you have some photos that you want to display in a larger format or maybe want to show off your picture taking talent, you can opt for a canvas print to display your photo as a piece of artwork.

Figure 6.16

Once you select your photo, you will have the same editing options that you are used to seeing throughout this book. Once everything looks the way you like, click on the *Use photo* button.

Then you will be prompted to choose a size and Photos will suggest a size for you based on the picture that you have chosen to use. Just keep in mind that the larger you go, the better quality\higher resolution your photo should be otherwise it might not come out as clear as you would like it to be.

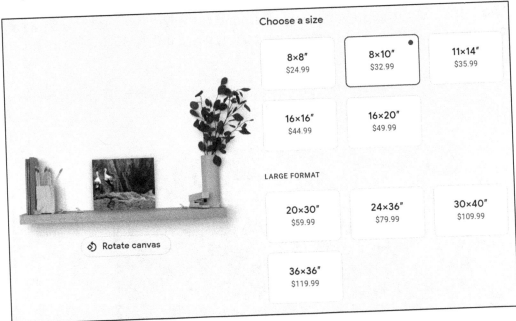

Figure 6.17

After you choose the size, you can then determine if you want the photo to wrap around the edges or if you want a simple black or white edge.

Figure 6.18

If you choose to have the photo wrap around the edges, you need to be aware that the edge of your picture might get cut off when it gets moved to the side of the canvas.

Figure 6.19

If this happens, you can use the edit function to move or crop your picture to make it fit as seen in figure 6.20.

Figure 6.20

Once you have everything looking the way you want, you can click on the 3D Preview slider to get a 3D view of how your photo canvas will look.

Figure 6.21

If everything looks good, you can then place your order.

Chapter 7 – Settings

When it comes to any type of software whether it be something you install on your computer or an application like Photos that you use online, I always like to check out the settings to see if there is anything that I can change to improve my experience when working with the software.

Google Photos has a settings section with quite a few options but once you take the time to check them out, you will see that they are fairly basic, but you still might find something you will want to tweak.

Even though all of the Photos settings are grouped together in one area. I will try and break them down into a few categories to help it make a little more sense.

General Settings

If you plan on uploading a large number of photos and don't want to pay for additional space, you can come here and choose the Storage saver option to have your images reduced to save space. If you are just going to be viewing and sharing your pictures, you probably won't notice any real difference in how they look. But if you plan on printing them and especially if you plan to do larger prints or the canvas option, you might want to leave them full size.

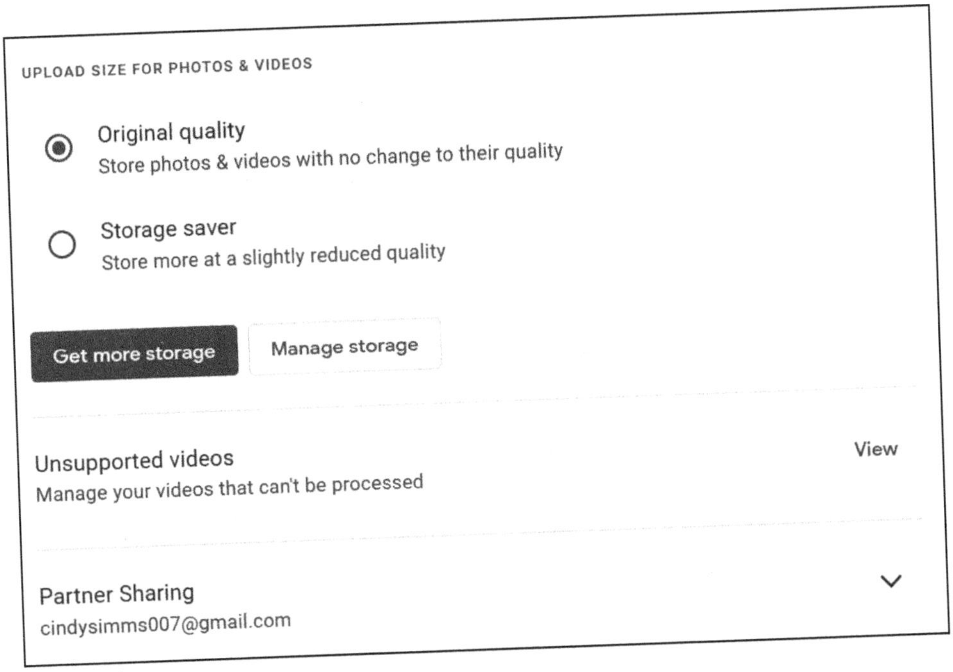

Figure 7.1

Google Photos does a pretty good job at playing most video formats, but you might have some videos that use a different format and are not viewable within your Photos account. If that is the case, you can go to the *Unsupported videos* setting and manage these videos or remove them to free up space in your account.

Photos supports most popular video formats such as .mpg, .mod, .mmv, .tod, .wmv, .asf, .avi, .divx, .mov, .m4v, .3gp, .3g2, .mp4, .m2t, .m2ts, .mts, and .mkv files.

If you are using the Partner sharing feature, you can come here to view the partner settings or remove a person if you don't want to share your photos with them any longer.

Partner Sharing
cindysimms007@gmail.com

    Google user
    cindysimms007@gmail.com

SHARED WITH CINDYSIMMS007@GMAIL.COM

cindysimms007@gmail.com can access

✓   All photos since Jan 1, 2020

✓   The location where your shared photos were taken. Learn more.

                        Remove partner

Figure 7.2

Preferences

The next group of settings I will be discussing covers some general preferences for your Photos account and you might want to come here to look things over to see if you need to make any changes.

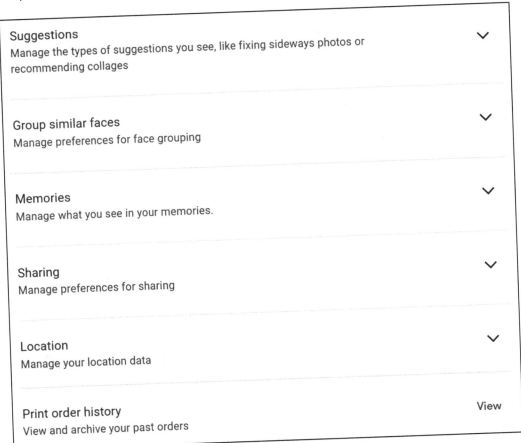

Figure 7.3

I will now give a brief description of what each of these settings can be used to adjust.

- **Suggestions** – You might have noticed how your computer and phone think they know what's best for you and are always trying to tell you what to do. Photos is no different and will make suggestions for things such as which photos you should archive, which photos would make a good collage, and how you should rotate your pictures to look their best.

   There is also an area where you can review past suggestions as well as view any creations you have previously worked on and never completed such as a photo album order.

- **Group Similar Faces** – You might recall that Photos will try and tag people's faces as well as your pet so you can group them together in albums etc. If you want to disable this feature, add your own face to be grouped based on one of your photos, or disable the pets grouping option, you can do so from here.

107

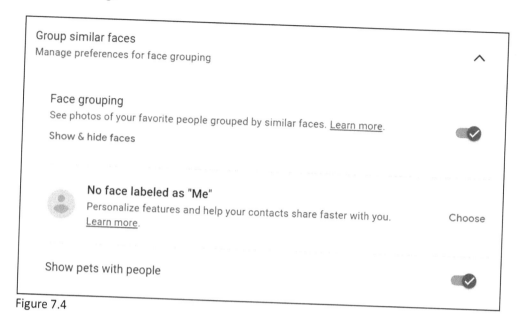

Figure 7.4

- **Memories** – One feature that Photos has is that it will create what it calls Memories from your photos and then give you the option to save them along with your other photos. It will do things such as make a collage from various images or add some type of filter effect to a photo and if you like it then you can use it as you like.

  There are many options here that you can configure such as hiding people, pets or dates if you don't want them to be used in one of these Memories. You can also disable certain features such as having it create collages, animations or stylized photos so that way you don't get any Memories created that you might not want.

- **Sharing** – There are only a couple of options that you can configure when it comes to how you share your pictures and videos. One of them is the ability to enable or disable notifications when you have new photos to share and the other is to hide video from your motion photos.

- **Location** – You saw earlier in the book how your camera will add location and other information to your photos assuming it's enabled so that way you will be able to see when and where the photo was taken. By default, Photos will use landmarks, location history and other sources to estimate where your photos were taken. If you don't want this to be applied to your photos, you can disable it here. You can also check your location history settings from your Google account from here and change them as needed.

- **Print order history** – If you have ordered any photo prints through Google Photos, you can view your order history from this section.

Email and Notifications

The next group is where you can enable or disable if or how often you get notified for particular events via email or a popup notification. Just like with most apps, Photos will let you know about things you may or may not care about. Fortunately, you can disable most of them if you feel you are getting bombarded with too much useless information.

There are three categories you can enable or disable as needed. The first one is if you have started a print order and then closed out Photos before completing the order. This is enabled by default but can easily be turned off.

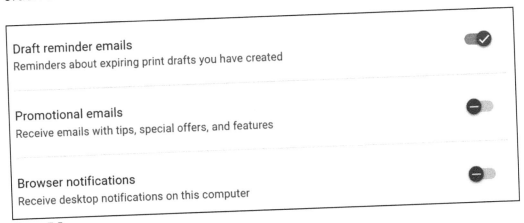

Figure 7.5

Then you have promotional emails which are disabled by default and for most of us that is a good thing! These are usually generic emails trying to get you to sign up for things or try out some features you might not normally use. If you want to see what kind of emails you will get with this, you can always enable it for a while and then if it gets to be too much, you can come back and disable it.

Browser notifications are popups that occur while you are in your Photos account online. They might include things such as someone sharing a file with you, or an album being updated etc. This is also disabled by default but can be turned on easily as well.

Backup and Logging

If you find that you are storing all of your pictures in Google Photos and not keeping a copy on your computer or phone, then you might get a little worried that you will end up losing all of your memories if something were to happen with your account.

Fortunately, there is a way to export all of your photos and videos to your PC as a backup so you have a copy that you can then put on an external hard drive or flash drive to lock them up and keep them safe.

From the *Export your data* section, you can start an export of all of your pictures and videos by following the process that I will now be going over.

Export your data	
Make a copy of your photos & videos, which you can use with a service outside of Google, or keep as an additional backup	∨
Your data in Google Photos	
Find out how we keep your photos & videos safe	View
Activity log	
View & remove your comments and messages on shared photos	View

Figure 7.6

Once you click on the down arrow to expand this section, you will then click on *Backup* to start the process. Then you can then make any changes as to what is going to be backed up if needed and then click on the *Next step* button.

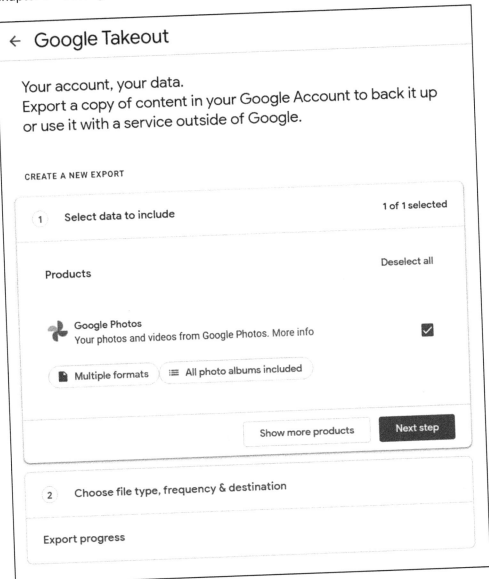

Figure 7.7

Under the Transfer to section, you can have Photos send you a link to download your data or you can have it sent to another online service such as Google Drive or DropBox. I will use the email link option and do a one time export. If you are a Windows user, I suggest keeping the file type as zip.

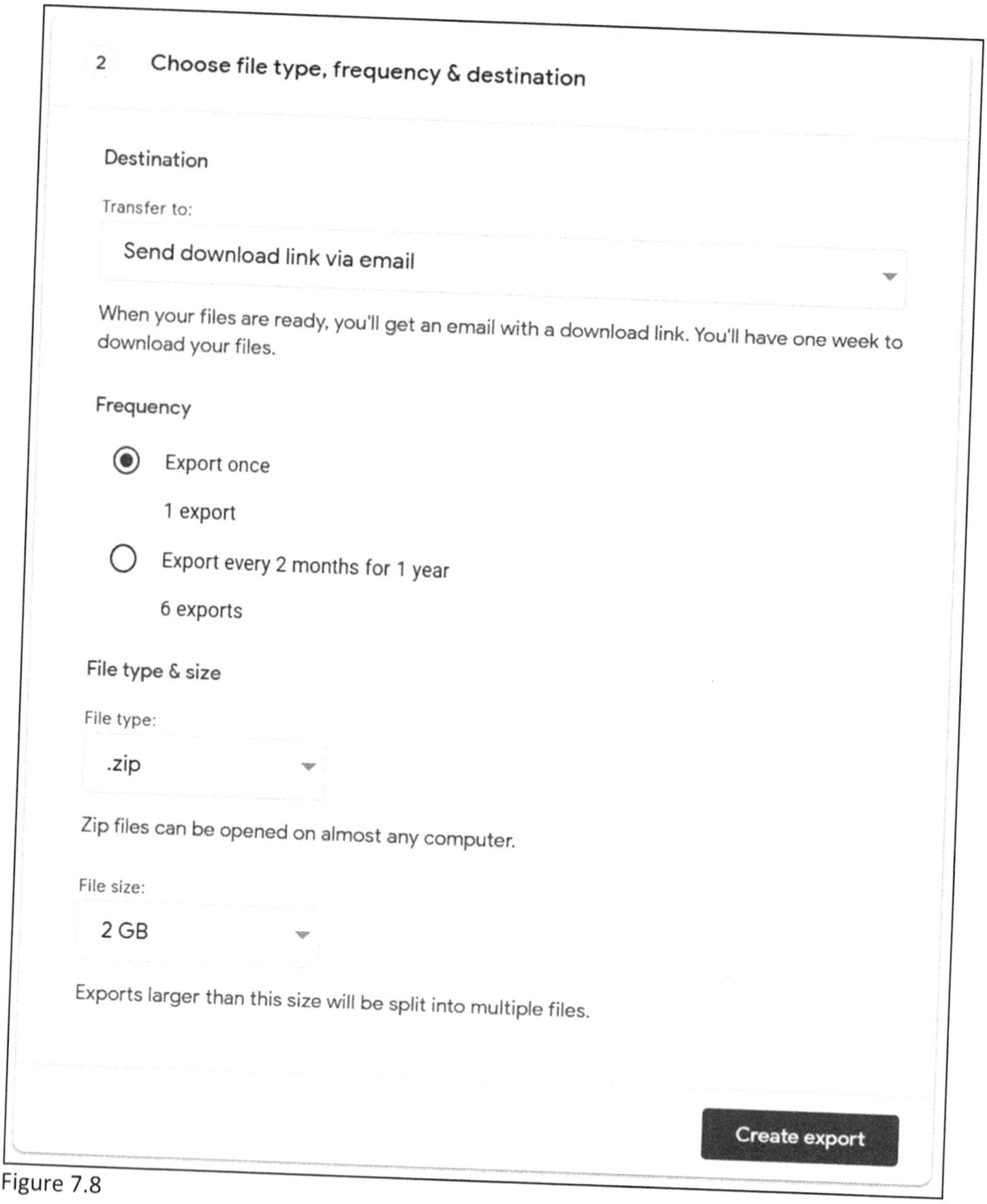

Figure 7.8

You will then see a message about your data being copied and preparing to be exported.

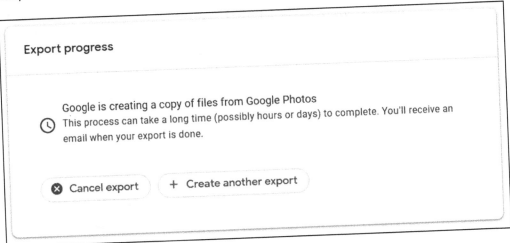

Figure 7.9

You will then receive an email with the subject of *Your Google data is ready to download* when the export is complete. When you open this email, you will have a button that says *Download your files*. This will take you to your Google Exports page and the zip file should start downloading automatically. If it doesn't, you can click on the *Download* button to start the download manually.

Once you extract the zip file, you will then see all of your pictures and albums grouped into specific folders. You will even have a copy of the items in your trash and information about any print orders you have placed.

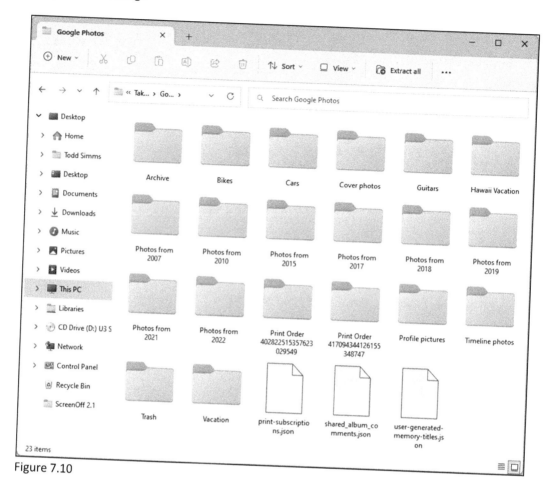

Figure 7.10

One last thing I wanted to mention from the setting section is the *Activity log*. Here you can view and\or remove any comments you have made on shared photos just in case you decided something wasn't appropriate or maybe you didn't word your comment the way you wanted to. Figure 7.11 shows a typical comments page and to remove a comment simply click on the X next to that comment.

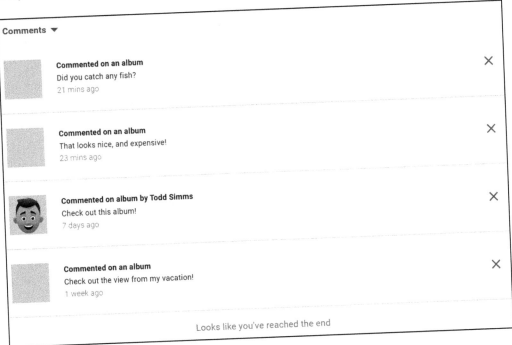

Figure 7.11

What's Next?

Now that you have read through this book and learned how to upload, edit and share your photos, you might be wondering what you should do next. Well, that depends on where you want to go. Are you happy with what you have learned, or do you want to further your knowledge on cloud storage or even photo editing by learning about how to use a more advanced program such as Adobe Photoshop?

If you do want to expand your knowledge, then you can look for some more advanced books that focus on cloud applications or online collaboration, if that's the path you choose to follow. Focus on mastering the basics, and then apply what you have learned when going to more advanced material.

There are many great video resources as well, such as Pluralsight or CBT Nuggets, which offer online subscriptions to training videos of every type imaginable. YouTube is also a great source for instructional videos if you know what to search for.

If you are content with being a proficient Photos user that knows more than your friends, then just keep on practicing what you have learned. Don't be afraid to poke around with some of the settings and tools that you normally don't use and see if you can figure out what they do without having to research it since learning by doing is the most effective method to gain new skills.

Thanks for reading **Google Photos Made Easy**. You can also check out the other books in the Made Easy series for additional computer related information and training. You can get more information on my other books on my Computers Made Easy Book Series website.

https://www.madeeasybookseries.com/

You should also check out my computer tips website, as well as follow it on Facebook to find more information on all kinds of computer topics.

www.onlinecomputertips.com
https://www.facebook.com/OnlineComputerTips/

About the Author

James Bernstein has been working with various companies in the IT field for over 20 years, managing technologies such as SAN and NAS storage, VMware, backups, Windows Servers, Active Directory, DNS, DHCP, Networking, Microsoft Office, Photoshop, Premiere, Exchange, and more.

He has obtained certifications from Microsoft, VMware, CompTIA, ShoreTel, and SNIA, and continues to strive to learn new technologies to further his knowledge on a variety of subjects.

He is also the founder of the website onlinecomputertips.com, which offers its readers valuable information on topics such as Windows, networking, hardware, software, and troubleshooting. James writes much of the content himself and adds new content on a regular basis. The site was started in 2005 and is still going strong today.